"Tom Geraty delivers his memoir, *Where the Trees Dance: A Memoir*, through the lens of amazing candor. This unfiltered directness is anchored by his candid understanding of mortal shortcomings coupled with a rare persistence to achieve. At times inspirational, at times uncomfortable, the searing honesty of his narrative is irresistible. With the stark, opening-passage imagery of facing every artist's fear – standing naked in front of the world – he instantly takes the reader to a relatable moment of truth. The release from an artist's mind into creation only becomes complete when the finished work is scrutinized by the world. Geraty's bold memoir challenges readers with a front row seat to a life filled with uncomfortable challenges, exhilarating triumphs, and a driving, first-person catharsis. Many memoirs stop short of how Geraty fully exposes his innermost thoughts, feelings and reactions to a world that shaped him, and his world that he shaped. Through his journey, each of us better understands others, and ourselves."

—John Busbee,
The Culture Buzz

"Tom Geraty takes us on a touching, personal journey. His nostalgic memoir weaves a story compelled by unconditional love: Love for his parents, his birth mother, his children – and most touchingly – his wife, Katie. Although a fine actor in his own right, it is through the roles of son, friend, lover, husband, and father that Geraty finally understands who he is and where he belongs. *Where the Trees Dance* evokes a simpler time before today's hyper-connected world. A time when parents trusted their kids to go out and experience life and let it take them wherever it may lead. Tom Geraty invites us along on his odyssey which ultimately leads him back to his one true love.

—Susan Woody, Director,
Des Moines Public Library

WHERE THE TREES DANCE

A MEMOIR

WHERE THE TREES DANCE

A MEMOIR

Tom Geraty

outskirts
press

Where the Trees Dance
A memoir and love song to a birth mother, mom and dad and the love of a life.
All Rights Reserved.
Copyright © 2023 Tom Geraty
v2.0

The opinions expressed in this manuscript are solely the opinions of the author and do not represent the opinions or thoughts of the publisher. The author has represented and warranted full ownership and/or legal right to publish all the materials in this book.

This book may not be reproduced, transmitted, or stored in whole or in part by any means, including graphic, electronic, or mechanical without the express written consent of the publisher except in the case of brief quotations embodied in critical articles and reviews.

Outskirts Press, Inc.
http://www.outskirtspress.com

ISBN: 978-1-9772-6241-7

Cover Photo © 2021 www.gettyimages.com. All rights reserved - used with permission.

Outskirts Press and the "OP" logo are trademarks belonging to Outskirts Press, Inc.

PRINTED IN THE UNITED STATES OF AMERICA

This is a love story, to adoption, birth mothers,
moms and dads, children, self-discovery,
and the love of a life…
disguised as a memoir.
For Rita, the woman who felt my first heartbeats.
For Moira and Tom, who chose me and raised me.
For Seamus and Graham, my sons,
my life's labor of love.
For Katie, my bride, my love.

All the events and experiences in this tale are true. I have changed the names of a few of the participants because we were just kids trying to find our way. If you recognize yourself, I mean no harm. I love what we were, and I love you, too.

Love and gratitude to cover designer Susan Bennett of Simple Truth, Chicago, for the beauty in your work and your life.

A tremendous thank you to proofreader/editor, Patrick McGill. With your brilliance and care, you turned this rough manuscript into the best version of itself. Next round is on me!

Special thanks to author rep. Lisa Buckley, and all the folks at Outskirts Press for all your expertise and care.

Many songs are mentioned throughout this memoir. A Spotify playlist has been created in the order of their appearance with the title "Where the Trees Dance," to enhance the reader's experience. If you like, cue up Dolores Keane's "Summer of My Dreams."

And away we go…

Prelude

Lights up on a nearly bare stage, with only a clothes-draped chair, a guitar, and a box or two of random props to be used as needed as the story unfolds. The pre-show music evolves into the beginning of Carly Simon's "Anticipation" playing loudly on a Bluetooth speaker from the wing offstage left, where also come the sounds of a shower running and a man singing along to the tune.

The sound of the shower ceases on Carly's first "Anticipation" chorus but the singing continues.

Paul Perquin, 61, enters from stage left with the lyric, "And I tell you, how easy it feels to be with you," naked, dripping, toweling off his body with his back to the audience. With some deft towel work, he works lyrics into his drying ritual. He wistfully observes his somewhat sagging butt cheeks in an imagined mirror upstage, turns full frontal to the audience.

Paul: When the hell did that happen?

Paul begins to dress...

1
Little Lad

I remember when my ass didn't sag. I would rather have the excess skin between my butt and upper hamstring removed by a plastic surgeon than have her carve off the folds of eyelid flesh that currently hang over my pupils like bean bags off the rim of a cornhole board and which, left unattended, will someday require I pull a drawstring to see. This, by the way, is an example of a kind of Idle Mental Moment a man can have while toweling off after a shower.

Which, by the way, is where I am, or rather, how I aim to be: naked. When I imagined writing a memoir in the days and weeks after learning about my birth mother, I believed I had to commit to two things: honesty and humor. If I wasn't willing to be 100% naked and honest, then why bother? And if I couldn't let myself laugh, or be laughed at, then why blather? For I am not a rock star, politician, movie star, athlete, inventor, or soldier. I am an ordinary man; truth and exposure are about all I have to give.

To put it another way, if you go to a vintage car dealership and are more drawn to the white Corvette convertible with red leather seats, you might not care to kick these tires. But if the partially restored '61 pickup with a little rust in the wheel wells, good upholstery, and original motor that starts in the morning and can work all day stops you in your tracks and makes you wonder where in the world it's been, then climb in, engage the clutch, and put this thing in gear.

I was born an orphan in 1961. My birth mother, a single woman abandoned by her "fiancé" (according to her family's lore), gave me up for adoption, over a thousand miles from her home and family. More about that later. But before she and I parted ways — was it an hour? a day? a week? — she made sure that I wasn't an orphan for long. Very soon I would be placed with a mom and dad that would prove to be the blessing of my life.

Apparently, the transition wasn't easy for me. My mom told me often enough so I couldn't forget, that I cried so hard and often as an infant that I gave myself a hernia. The scar, ever so faint, remains to this day from the repair, as do the echoes of those cries, which creaked through the core of my being for more than 30 years like wood beams around the walls of some forsaken mine.

Here's a random list of a few things I did before I turned twelve:

- Destroyed a neighbor's mailbox with an M-80 firecracker.
- Masturbated.
- Smoked a cigarette (not after the former).
- Had a girl's bubble gum-flavored tongue in my mouth.
- Was a serial shoplifter.
- Established myself as the fastest kid in the neighborhood.
- Was punched in the face multiple times during fights.

- Rode in the backseat of a police car.
- Earned my own pocket money.

And it occurs to me that a few of these might be worthy of some elaboration, a glimpse into the life of a free spirited, self-assured Midwestern boy.

"THOU SHALT NOT STEAL!"

I was a God-fearing, Jesus, Mary and Joseph loving, six day a week churchgoing, scapular-wearing, priest-respecting, Catholic school boy and future altar boy about to break one of the Ten Commandments. What force on earth could make me do that? For Christ and Mary's sake, I often fell asleep with rosary beads in my hands in those days.

In one word: Mattel. Or maybe, Harry.

I mean, how badly did I need another Hot Wheels car? On my First Communion, my mom wrapped a dozen Matchbox cars for me to open when I got home from mass. By the time I reached the age of ten I'd amassed a huge collection of those and Hot Wheels. Why steal another one? It had to be Harry.

Now, I hate to throw Harry under the school bus we rode together for eight years. We were best friends! We were literally blood brothers after cutting our thumbs with a pocketknife and pressing them together for several seconds in third grade. But he is the common denominator in three of the most guilt-producing and confessional-worthy episodes of my childhood. And so, as our innocent ages were waning and our inseparable paths ever so slowly coursed into different worlds, before that schism was complete, we stole.

First, we each stole a sew-on patch from the hobby store. What did I need a sew-on patch for, and how in the hell was I going to sew it on? My mom was still darning socks in those days and had the skills to handle a patch, but I wasn't going to ask her to sew on a patch I'd stolen and risk lying about where I got it. So, I hid it in a drawer in a side table no one used in the family room. A few days later, emboldened by success, Harry and I each liberated a Matchbox car from the Kmart toy department. I went home and, like a budding hoarder/thief, hid the car with the patch.

The third time was not a charm. Back at the Kmart, I took a sweet Hot Wheels car over to a rack of coats. Whilst pretending to peruse the garments, I removed the car from its bulky packaging and put the car in my pocket. Then, in a move that put the loin in purloin and the hot in Hot Wheel, I let the packaging fall to the floor rather than hide it in a coat pocket like Harry had done. Did I want to get caught, or what? Mine was a careless, rookie move that resulted in the store's inventory control specialist meeting us outside the main exit and escorting us to a back room where we waited for a policeman. Then, after phone calls home, our moms arrived to take us home.

Mom told me I was grounded for a week and sent me to my room to wait until my dad got home. Being sent to my room wasn't much of a punishment, what with my Mad Magazines, baseball encyclopedia, and radio for company. When the time came, dad didn't say much. He rarely did. He knew that I knew stealing was wrong. And besides, the guilt an Irish mother could lay on a boy was enough to slay any demon. I never stole again. When my mom and dad left my room that evening, it may have been the first of many times they said, "We don't think you should be playing with Harry anymore."

There are two things I could do better than anyone in my neighborhood and in my grade at school: win a foot race and throw a snowball at a moving object. It is the former that would be dispelled a couple years later by a girl you'll soon meet named Pam in a race in front of the recently built department store, Richman Gordman, the damn construction of which wiped out a full half of my childhood frontier on the other side of the creek. The latter resulted in Harry's and my escort home in a police car.

First, a few thoughts about throwing snowballs at cars. I am so fortunate that no accidents occurred as a result of my well-timed projectiles' collisions with the quarter panels, doors, windows and roofs of hundreds of cars, delivery vans, milk trucks, semis and buses over a roughly three-year career.

But goddamnit I was good at it!

So much goes into being successful. Residential areas are tricky, but also the most fun. A boy must first find locations to throw from that, ideally, meet the following criteria: on a street with just enough traffic to make it dodgy to pull over; between two houses where nobody is home; evergreen shrubbery near the foundation no less than four feet tall; perhaps on a curved road; no close street at the flank or rear (where an offended motorist could conveniently pull over and surprise you); and an excellent escape route. In addition, fresh snow must be trampled in several directions to prevent tracking when running from a launch area.

I vividly recall my favorite location in Windsor Heights, Iowa, on the south side of College Drive where the road curves between 78th and 79th Streets. It met all the above criteria. In addition, there was a large evergreen tree near the sidewalk which meant a driver never knew what hit them. My escape route was genius, in amid a cluster of short evergreen bushes at the back corner of the very house I threw from, just 25 feet away.

Oh my God, there was nothing in my young life that offered the exhilaration of a well-thrown snowball into the side panel of a car or truck, the thud of impact, the flash of brake lights and the screech of tires on pavement! If we saw the vehicle back up, we ran.

It happened at the location I mentioned. I ran 25 feet, crawled into the bushes, wedged myself between the branches and house, and tried to control my breathing. I waited. I listened. I saw the feet run past and heard them pause. I likely heard swearing and shouts of, "Where'ya at, you little shits!?" Had he searched the bushes I'd have been toast and most likely beaten to a pulp. No one who backed up a car on a curve, left the motor running and the door open, and gave chase to a couple of punk hooligans was going to be content with a word or two of admonition. A guy like my dad keeps driving. Dudes that back up and park want blood.

So that was the thrill we sought. And we were never caught! Most of the time, when challenged, we'd head to a predetermined rendezvous, another yard perhaps or a participant's garage or basement with an outside door we knew was unlocked and where the thrill dissipated in laughter and warmth and safety. The tale would last for days.

We threw from yards, parks, creeks, even our hilltop churchyard on University Avenue when evening altar boy meetings let out early and we waited for our fathers to come pick us up (churches make great hideouts!). But like most miscreants who do something too well for too long, Harry and I got careless.

We broke our own rule and decided that throwing snowballs from atop a hill, in the parking lot of a motel across from that Richman Gordman looking down on the busy four lane Hickman Road that re-emerged as Highway 6 west of town, was a good idea. We figured that if we got chased, we could run to the nearby woods and creek and disappear.

We were having a ball, a snowball! We were nailing cars and trucks from 80 feet away, leading them as well as a quarterback ever led a receiver on a crossing route in any high school football game we'd ever seen. And there were no defenders... until police from three adjoining communities, Windsor Heights, Urbandale and Clive, converged at once. We ran.

Harry made it to the woods but I stopped. There was no escaping this time. It was quickly determined where I lived, I was put in a police car and very easily convinced to give up my buddy. I told the officer that Harry was probably making his way through the woods that lined the creek behind some houses that led to our neighborhood. Sure enough, they found him and put him in the seat beside me. We were driven and deposited at the front door of our respective houses where our moms were probably making supper. I was sent to my room and told to wait until my dad got home, grounded for a month. A month! It appeared that throwing snowballs at cars was worse than breaking a Ten Commandment, and I have to wonder now, half a century later, if this wasn't the first dent in my Catholic belief.

That same creek and woods, that once-upon-a-time thriving vibrant ecosystem whose waters I literally drank from, is where I smoked my first cigarette. Harry lifted a couple of Benson & Hedges out of his mom's purse and we lit up while sitting on a tree that had fallen across the creek. It made for a fantastic bridge. As a site for the initiation rites into the mysteries of tobacco? Not so much.

I took a puff and inhaled like all my aunts and uncles (except Aunt Betty who added to her habit the bizarrely fascinating trait of sticking out her tongue every time she inhaled), coughed and repeated several times. Quite a nice little moment for two young boys; these were the days when minnows, crawdads and tadpoles actually lived in the creek and swam beneath our feet; butterflies abounded; birds sang in yonder trees and taunted the barking squirrels; deer that ravaged our parents' gardens at night hid nearby; it was like a somewhat darker Norman Rockwell painting, perhaps truer. I might have become a lifelong smoker if I hadn't stood up and immediately fell off the log into the creek. Who knew tobacco made one dizzy? I didn't, obviously.

As a side note, I fell into that creek too many times to recall, such that the smell of creek water on a child's drying clothes is one of the rare keys to the vault wherein my inner child resides. I recognized it instantly when, many years later, I could smell it on my own boy's clothes upon their return home after catching frogs and tadpoles at the Greenwood Park pond. I am ever so grateful for the childhood I had. My pals and I roamed our world unfettered and unfenced, with full license to cross any yard without fear or question en route to our Walnut Creek wilderness. It is one of those paradoxes of my youth, where an experience is only truly beautiful because I didn't know it at the time.

If the rosary was a prayer one said to honor events of their childhood and youth rather than the life of Mary and Jesus, we would, no doubt, still have Sorrowful

Mysteries, Joyful Mysteries and Glorious Mysteries. (And by the way, when did they add the Luminous Mysteries?) For example, one of the Sorrowful Mysteries might be "Jamie (androgynous name) is Mollified by a Pacifier." A Joyful Mystery might be "Jamie Poops in a Toilet for the First Time (also a Parental Joyful Mystery)." A Glorious Mystery would have to be "Jamie Walks for the First Time."

But I KNOW what the Third Luminous Mystery of the Child/Youth Rosary is: "The First Kiss." Tommy's lips are touched for the first time by something other than food, drink, the fists of neighborhood boys and schoolmates, or well-intentioned but farsighted moms, aunts, and grandmas.

That seems lacking.

The First Kiss: Rachel takes the bubble gum out of her mouth and places her soft, wet lips upon Tommy's, pulls away and asks, "Have you ever French kissed?"

Correction. The Third Luminous Mystery: "The Second Kiss."

After a brief tutorial, Tommy's lips part, Rachel puts her tongue in his mouth, finds his, and his head explodes.

I'm pretty sure I was too young to have an erection, so there was no embarrassing body language, nothing to hide, as we timed our exits from the stage door a minute-or-so apart and I wafted down the hallway to the music room.

It was fifth grade. I was ten years old. And I know for a fact that it was Rachel's idea that we kiss. Of course, I liked her. What boy didn't? She was so pretty, with her long brown hair and big brown eyes. She was more athletic than most of the boys in fifth grade, and three times more mature. But I never dreamed of actually kissing that queen. How I became one of her drones remains a mystery to this day. A Luminous Mystery, indeed. It must have gone something like this: Her equally mature friend, Pam, approached me one day on the playground and asked, "Would you like to kiss Rachel?" I'm sure I blushed, then said, "Yes."

Arrangements were made that Rachel and I would meet for this kiss behind the curtains in what I'd come to learn later was the stage right wing of the school stage, closest to the hallway that led from the church hall to the music room. Understand that music class was held across the parking lot from the school, in the basement of the church in a room across from the kitchen which served the church hall/gymnasium, at one end of which was the stage where school plays and concerts were performed. Because of the distance from the main school to the church, we had a little extra time.

It was magical really. It was fifth grade. I was holding Rachel close to me like I'd seen on TV. Feeling her body, her lips, her tongue! For crying out loud! I was a mess. Was this love? Was she my girlfriend? Why me? Why not me?

It was the first of many rendezvous, and soon Pam was involved. Locations varied: the stage, the back of the darkened classroom during a filmstrip or movie, the coat closet, the janitor's closet between the girl's and boy's restroom, even the crying room in the church at the top of the stairs just down the hallway from the music room in the other direction! I think the only constant was the taste of bubble gum and a rapid heart rate.

These adventures mostly faded away by the end of sixth grade. By then, I was kissed more often and had touched more breasts than I would in all my years of high school. I know, pathetic, and a little weird when viewed beyond the early 70's era blacklight of Pam's basement, but no less dear.

The episode of "The First Kiss" is on the Mount Rushmore of my grade school memories. Up there would be my fourth-grade teacher, Mrs. Maher. Being an altar boy ranks high. And just the cumulative highs and lows of experiencing a Catholic education with mostly the same group of friends and classmates for eight years.

That is a "Rushmore," so I suppose the time in seventh grade when I beat up an eighth grader by throwing him over a row of desks like I was in a scene from "Bonanza" won't make the mountain. Anyway, that fight does not belong amidst the hallowed realm of "The First Kiss." Rather, it resides in the visitor's center of the life I lived for two years after learning that I was adopted: "The Angry Years."

Conscience: Whoa, whoa, whoa, whoa, whoa! You can't stroke our curiosity by mentioning masturbation in a list of pre-twelve accomplishments and not elaborate.

Me: Ahhh. Ummmm.

Conscience: That's like saying you flew your buddies to a nude beach in Greece and only brought one pair of Ray-Bans.

Me: What? Anyway, now it kinda feels too personal.

Conscience: You brought it up.

Me: What was I thinking?

Conscience: You tell me, and anyone who might be reading.

Me: I was simply making a list of some things that maybe should have happened AFTER I was eleven or twelve.

Conscience: I see. To pound the point home.

Me: Hilarious.

Conscience: Am I rubbing you the wrong way?

Me: You're not funny. This is awkward.

Conscience: I understand. This is a topic that requires a delicate touch.

Me: One more time and I'm turning you off! I'm serious!

Conscience: Serious? All right. All right. Seriously, don't be serious! Here's an idea: there's nothing like a well-placed sports metaphor to get the juices flowing.

Me: Damnit! I told you…

Conscience: Hear me out. You use them all the time. And they work. They work with your wife, at your job, teaching your sons a life lesson. Just try it. Break the ice, go for gold, cast your line, lace 'em up, and of course, step up to the plate.

Me: You mean something like, "Batting lead-off for the Prepubescent Discoverers, Tommy Geraty"?

Conscience: (Must I do everything?) It would be a few years before Tommy really found his stroke and was swinging it in the Bigs, hitting clean-up for teams like the Sinners, the Spankers, the Wankers, the Chicken Chokers, Jerkers, Jackers and for a couple seasons in Ireland late in his career, the Tossers.

Me: Okay. Okay. I got it from here.

Those innocent, carefree days in the A League. It isn't even masturbation. It's just a sensation, something that feels good. For a boy, and a girl I suppose, it isn't much different than being tickled.

The first time I felt that sensation in the place where my pee came from, I was probably climbing something:

a tree, a tetherball pole, a basketball pole. Kids climb. And when boys climb, sometimes it creates a sensation that feels good and bears repeating on occasion.

To be clear, not every tree climbed or pole shimmied produced that feeling. Much has to do with one's intention. As far as trees are concerned, they are more like mountains to kids, or pirate ships, and not objects of hidden pleasure.

For example, we had a tree in the neighborhood that I swear nature designed as the perfect tree for a kid to climb. This tree was a palpable presence in my life for four or five years.

I'd pass it on my way home from kindergarten at the public elementary in the neighborhood and marvel as the older kids climbed to its highest nooks like sailors to a crow's nest. At that time, I couldn't reach the tree's lowest limb, not even by jumping, its height like a barrier for those too young or weak to safely board. Almost every day on my way home from kindergarten I'd jump as I passed, stretching ever so closer to a touch of that branch. Later, in the summer and subsequent earliest school years when I bussed to the Catholic elementary, I made less-frequent pilgrimages to that tree to measure my prowess.

Here is a little story of my last day in kindergarten that I love to recall. It just makes me chuckle, and in light of this memoir, sheds some meaning on a tendency that remained throughout my life: that of living in the moment.

I walked out of Miss McLish's classroom laden with my crayons, school supplies and nap rug to begin the seven-block walk home, far too burdened for a five-year-old newly freed from the rigors of staying within the lines and connecting the dots. When I came to the College Drive bridge spanning Walnut Creek, not quite halfway between 73rd and 80th, I threw everything over the rail into the water below. Everything. When mom asked me where my things were when I got home, I told her I threw them in the creek because I was through with school and wouldn't need them anymore. I don't recall getting in trouble. I think my mom found it as funny as I do now. Even though there was a precedent in my family of continuing education, my older sister was in third grade after all, to me it was summer and first grade never entered my mind.

Or perhaps I was thinking that, as a kindergarten graduate, I would now have the strength to climb that tree. How could I do that while carrying snub-nosed scissors and a bottle of Elmer's glue?

"Yup, I don't need THESE anymore. Time to go get a snack and play!"

At any rate, that tree was indeed my growth chart. Many months passed before my rite of passage was earned, when I could jump beneath that lowest limb, hook one hand over the top, hold on long enough to steady myself, swing my other hand up and over the other side, hook my fingers, walk my feet up the trunk, swing one leg over the branch and follow that momentum as I worked my body up and over to the skyward side where I sat up proud, my back against the trunk.

I made it! Getting into that tree was my greatest physical achievement since learning to ride a bike, perhaps greater because I did it on my own. The rest was easy. The tree provided the perfect succession of steps and holds and crannies to safely ascend to its highest reaches. Ahoy to the greatest tree a boy could want! I must pay it a visit next time I'm in my old neighborhood. I wonder if it's still there. Some of those innermost rings know me well.

But back to the playground. Out there, a boy can run out at recess and, in the shadow of the church steeple, pull himself up the tetherball pole for ten or fifteen seconds, then run off and join the kickball game a tad wobbly kneed. To me, it was just natural. Out there in the open. Nothing to hide. No doubt, classmates and older kids who'd experienced the same sensation saw me and didn't think twice. I was never teased.

Of course, at some point we stop climbing poles, right? You wouldn't want to be in fifth grade and knocking off a quick thirty seconds up the basketball pole on the way to confessions.

It's funny the things I remember, like the time my family was visiting our cousins when I was barely out of the A League. I went down to the basement where all the boys slept, and there was my younger cousin, Tammy, riding almost trance-like up and down the stair railing like a yo-yo on a short string. I knew what was happening, I'd ridden a handrail or two, but I was like, "Whatever."

I don't know how long the "whatever" era lasted for me, several months for sure, maybe two or three years? But I sure remember my final at bat in the A League.

One day, a few months prior to that promotion, my good friend, Kevin, asked me, "You want to feel something cool?" or something like that. I said, "Sure, why not," or something like that.

So, he proceeded to show me how, if I reached over the narrow kitchen counter and grabbed on to the other side, then raised my knees into a kind of fetal position and pressed them against the backside of the cabinet and spread my knees in and out in rapid succession, it produced a nice feeling. I tried it. It felt like climbing a pole.

And that was that. We played dozens of games at Kevin's house. They had a trampoline. We watched TV, played records, kicked footballs. Everything seemed to center in Kevin's backyard for several years of my childhood, and once in a while I visited his kitchen.

My final at bat in the minors came in Kevin's kitchen. Maybe I should say it "happened," not "came"? In any case, you can imagine what occurred. I'm working my knees like windshield wipers in a hurricane when, in a moment that was at once exhilarating and frightening, I came in my shorts. I went immediately to their guest bathroom to see what had just happened, and very quickly decided I needed to phone my agent. I went straight home (call it a walk-off) and made the call.

And for the record (what's a good baseball metaphor without records?), I had a fair few at bats in the Big Leagues before The Angry Years. Most, if not all, resulted in walk-offs. The pitchers ranged from the wholesome hurlers in the lingerie section of my mom's Sears catalog, to the southpaws in a contraband Playboy, to the batting practice fast balls I discovered one day in my dad's calendar sample cases. I have to share that story.

My dad sold funeral supplies to funeral homes all over the state of Iowa, everything from caskets to memorial books to prayer cards to religious calendars. For a while, I recall he even sold embalming fluids. I remember the company that supplied his calendars, Superior Gift Line (the things one remembers).

My dad used to give me calendar samples from the previous year's case once the new line arrived: twelve months of mountain views, wildlife, lighthouses, birds, etc. I'd make collages sometimes. I'd tape them to my bedroom door. It was beautiful photography. One day during what might have been my rookie season in the Big Leagues, I went into my dad's office to look through the new year's sample case.

Oh, my sweet taatooties! There were three or four sections of nude calendars! Most had twelve months, some six! Various sizes! In history class we were learning about the settling of the American West and I now truly understood how John Sutter felt when he found that nugget of gold in California. Need I say more? Suffice to say, the guest bathroom down the hall from dad's office became my home field, my friendly confines, my very own Wrigley Field! Batter up!

2
"Yesterday Once More"

The innocent age of this story is passing. Must it? May I linger a while longer? What an utterly blissful time was had by this Midwestern child in the innocent age. I fully understand how privileged and blessed I was to grow up where I did, on the fringe of a fair-sized city, with a boyhood wilderness of woodland, creek, and farms beyond the end of my street. With a mom and dad that loved unconditionally, shared selflessly, provided beautifully. With a mom that saw me off to school every day and was there every day when I came home. I'm pretty sure I learned everything I needed to know to raise my own two sons during my innocent age.

But move on I must.

Dan Fogelberg titled an album "The Innocent Age." There is a song on that album called "The Sand and the Foam" in which he wrote, "Gone are the pathways the child followed home, gone like the sand and the foam." In my case, that is literally true. My wilderness became a department store and hundreds of houses and townhomes. The creek remains, but I'd be sick for days if I slaked my thirst cowboy style from its banks like I did so deliciously then. If I walked through the trees and up the hill from the creek into the familiar back yards today, I'd be suspicious at best.

And yet, the pathways are there for me in my heart, in my mind. I remember every one of them! I'm not afraid or embarrassed to visit them there from time to time. There is no suspicion in my heart when I visit my childhood. How lucky I am! How welcome I am there! Those pathways are a cherished part of me that lead to an utterly joyous time before time existed for me.

    I was headed to one of those pathways in the summer of 1973, a few weeks before my twelfth birthday. I might have been headed to Dan's house for a home run derby game, or maybe to shoot some baskets. It was out the back sliding door, through three backyards, over a chain linked fence, under a redwood-stained panel fence, and I was in Dan's backyard. Or maybe I was simply headed over to Kevin's, out the back slider and down the tiny hill, two doors down, to jump on the trampoline or chip golf balls against the tree in his front yard. He was Julius Boros, I was Lee Trevino.

    Wherever I was going that late afternoon (it was cocktail hour), it was through the family room where my mom and dad were sitting and watching the news. Before I got to the sliding patio door, my mom said they wanted to talk to me. They asked me to sit down. I did a quick rewind in my mind of my most recent endeavors and was pretty sure I wasn't in trouble. I sat down in the orange vinyl 60's era swivel chair next to that table that once housed my shoplifting booty and waited.

    "Your father and I wanted to tell you that you were adopted."

    That's all I remember hearing. I sat there for a minute, stunned. I'm pretty sure they told me how much they loved me and how this didn't change anything and how I was adopted as a baby and how my older sister was also adopted and how after I was adopted, they were able to have my younger sister and that she wasn't adopted.

I do remember being asked if I had any questions. I said I didn't. After an awkward pause, I asked if I could go out and play. Mom probably said something like, "Of course you can. Dinner is in half an hour."

I went outside.

I've forgotten where I went or what I did for that half hour. I might have just gone to one of my quiet spots, behind the lilac bushes on the north side of the house, or on the cement steps at the back of the garage that led down to the basement. It was those stairs where I would later drink my first beer, a can of Falstaff lifted out of my dad's beer fridge. It was those stairs where, earlier, I once kissed a neighbor girl, the younger sister of my good friend, Kevin, who, somewhat oddly, arranged the whole affair. (Marilyn, if that was your First Kiss, I apologize. It was nothing more than a somewhat prolonged meeting of closed lips.)

If this were a work of fiction, I would create an entire mythic chapter around those thirty odd minutes I spent between learning of my adoption and sitting down at the dinner table. How I walked, stunned, over to Kevin's backyard where every kid in the neighborhood had congregated around the trampoline like so many other summer afternoons. How suddenly I was different than every other kid I knew. How the weight of telling a boy that he was adopted was suddenly shifted from the shoulders of my mom and dad into this invisible ball and chain wrapped around my mind and chest. How I would never play organized baseball again. How the ensuing hours, days, weeks, months, and years of ignorance and avoiding any further talk on the subject would cement my sense that I was strange, and send me on a decades long quest to understand where in the hell I fit in. Oh wait, that's what happened.

Myths. Quests. Heroes. Well, if it's true that we are all the heroes of our own life story, then okay, I've read Joseph Campbell. I know the archetype of how a normal life leads the hero to a challenge and a call to action and yadda yadda yadda. I knew none of that then. I felt as heroic as a puffy white cumulus cloud in a blue July sky: nice on the outside, but within were the makings of a storm set to blow just beyond the horizon.

3
The Angry Years

In so many ways, my mom and dad were right, nothing changed. When I sat down to the family dinner that evening, not a word was spoken about adoption. The same would hold true for the tens of thousands of breakfasts, lunches and dinners and encounters brief and long over the next twenty or so odd years. I finally broke the silence in my early thirties by asking my mom why we never talked about my adoption. She replied, "We thought you didn't want to talk about it."

Oh my God. What could I say to that? It sure wasn't the answer I expected. I asked my mom why she always turned off the TV whenever an adoption story came on the news. In my early teens we got a small TV for the kitchen, and it played the local news during supper. She replied that she thought it upset me.

Okay, I let it go. My dad was buried on my 34th birthday and my mom passed away when I was 41. We never talked about my adoption again. But I'm getting ahead of myself.

I didn't know that the next two years, seventh and eighth grade, would be "The Angry Years." I didn't know that testosterone was flying out of my balls like buckshot into my brain and bones and muscles and fists. I know, a lot of boys go through puberty without getting into fights and raising Cain. (Part of me just wanted to write "out of my balls like buckshot." It won out over "out of my testicles like ticker tape.") But if I mix puberty with my rapidly growing sense of my differentness, with no other outlet to vent the turbulence of having my worldview rocked in ways I couldn't bestill, with no answers to my simplest questions because the two people I loved more than anyone, my mom and dad, fell silent and blind, then, in my case, a bully was born.

I'm not proud of it. It was the worst two years of my life. And I'm glad I got it out of my system when I did; twelve- and thirteen-year-old fists don't hurt that bad. I know because a fair few landed on my own face. Whatever, I'm just glad The Angry Years didn't happen when I was 22.

My memory is one of my most cherished possessions. If it ever goes away, in that slow Alzheimer's dementia kind of way, I am certain I will end my life before I lose it all. I'm not being morose. It's a thought that gives me great comfort, knowing that I won't be a burden if my light goes out along with an ability to wipe my own ass. Read this story to its end and you'll perhaps understand that I'm at a place in my life where death isn't scary.

I remember a single summer day when I was five or six years old. The twin girls from across the street and I spent the better part of an hour in my side yard by the lilac bushes, lying in the grass, trying to draw perfect circles on white paper with colored pencils. That lovely moment ended when their mom called them home. I don't think she could see us from their front porch.

I remember, maybe a year later, being dropped off at the Plaza Theater adjacent to Merle Hay Mall with my friend Gary to see the latest Disney movie while my mom shopped. The boy next to me shared his bucket of popcorn. It wasn't my first encounter with an African American (there were a few families in our parish, though none in my grade), but it was by far my closest. He shared that tub of popcorn like I was his brother, and I'd like to think that it was my friend for two hours who won the day when, a handful of years later, my dad referred to black folks as "shines" and I understood it was wrong.

But I'm thinking now about the times and memories of those I bullied. It pains me to think that if I can recall moments like those I just described, experienced at an earlier age, devoid of pain and trauma, how vivid must be the memory of the younger boy I tackled to the ground, sat upon his chest and punched in the face, not once but twice, just because he cut through my yard on his way home?

The twin girls soon moved away and a family with three younger boys moved in across the street. One day, the oldest one called me "Tammy" (that's what my name sounded like when my dad called me home) and I bloodied his nose.

The fights at school were epic. I mentioned the Bonanza-style brawl in Mrs. Brown's seventh grade social studies classroom that ended with me throwing Earl Wilson over a row of desks. Fights inside were rare. Most fights were outside on the playground. Tempers flared from an injustice perpetrated, shoving ensued, and before Sister Slaphappy knew what was going on, a circle formed around the combatants and fists were flying amidst a chorus of "Fight! Fight! Fight!"

In one such fight, I had Frank Harrison on the ground in a headlock, alternating knees to the ribs and trying to land face shots with my fist. He went limp. A few of our classmates pulled me off. I didn't know he had asthma. Thankfully, he had his inhaler. Chances are a kid with asthma wouldn't pick a fight. I think I was an ass.

I didn't win all my fights. Bolstered by my win in the Wilson brawl, I took on another eighth grader over a dispute about possession of a keep-away ball. I challenged him. I swung and missed. He immediately landed a right hook to my jaw that dropped me like a sour half pint carton of milk. The fight was over before it began.

I was disrespectful to my teachers. I got under the 6'8" skin of Mr. Bauman so deeply that he dragged me out of the classroom and across the hall, the nape of my neck in his hand like a basketball, to the stairwell where he picked me up by my belt and neck and pressed me against the coat hooks. I'm surprised there's not an effigy of me impaled there to this day as a reminder to kids what happens when you talk back to a teacher. (I know there is no memorial to my mischief because I was a substitute teacher at that school for a few weeks in my middle fifties and lingered in that stairwell long enough to evoke my ghosts, tell them I love them, and smile.)

I once drove the normally meek Sister Donna to such a state of ire in eighth grade that she screamed in front of the entire class, "You'll never have any friends!" Things were trending in that direction.

I could go on for pages, but I'll end with the episode that brings me more pain and shame and regret than any other in my life. Over the span of a few weeks, a couple other boys and I tormented the smallest and weakest girl in our class. There were times we closed her in the coat closet in the back of the room. We hit her.

It breaks my heart and knots my stomach to remember, and yet for those few weeks we must have haunted her much more than this memory haunts me. If I believed in heaven, I honestly don't think there would be a place for me there. Finally, her mother went to the teachers, who then went to my parents. A meeting was held at the school. Apologies expressed. Wrists slapped. And that was it. I swear to God if those teachers and nuns had had their heads out of their asses or their asses out of their teacher's lounge, just paying the least bit of attention, they might have spared Dorothea that pain and smacked my punk ass up one side of St. Theresa's School and down the other. I deserved it.

I was so mean and angry in those two years. It didn't even matter that my mom volunteered at the school and knew all the teachers. I was losing myself in the worst way. It is not hyperbole to say that a battle was being waged in my soul between the boy I was and the adolescent I would become. And by soul, I mean the one that, in those days, I very much believed belonged to God. I still prayed the rosary in my bed at night. I went to mass six days a week. I confessed my sins!

Going to confession at the age of twelve and thirteen was two days of turmoil, leading up to two minutes of agony, followed by a half hour of rapture.

We had confessions every First Friday, the day every boy was required to wear a tie to school (as if the holy noose around my neck wasn't tight enough already). This meant that on Wednesday of that week, I would begin to agonize over needing to confess to masturbating because I now understood how sinful and shameful and wrong it was and how disappointed God was in me.

Who am I kidding? I felt that guilt and shame every time I "rubbed one out," and not just for two days before confessions. Add to that the fact that I'd have to admit this grievous act to the very priest that told all of us how sinful it was! I was an altar boy! He knew my voice!

Thus, the lead-up to going to confession with that grave sin staining my conscience was akin to someone with a beachfront home watching the approaching path of a hurricane on the Weather Channel. Every First Friday for two years, a storm hit the shore of my soul. I only mustered up the courage to save it a couple times. (What a relief it would be to learn that confession was optional in high school.)

At any rate, it began something like this:

"Bless me Father for I have sinned. These are my sins: I dishonored my mother and father four times. I hit my sister for going into my room. I masturbated. I got into three fights. I said the Lord's name in vain on the playground twice." Notice how I sneaked it in there?

It ended something like this:

"That's a good confession. Say two Our Fathers and three Hail Marys and go with God. Now let's hear a good Act of Contrition."

Oh my God, I am heartily sorry for having offended thee! I'm pure again! I'm saved! I can look at the figure up there on the cross in the eyes, from my kneeler while I say my penance, without shame! In all honesty, the feeling I had those two or three times I fully confessed my sins was as sublime as any I had in all of my first thirteen years of life.

It lasted about as long as it took to walk across the parking lot from the church back to the school. Once there, someone might cut the line at the drinking fountain and elicit an expletive or shove, or a girl might sit across from me, forget to sit like a lady, expose her underwear, elicit an impure thought and wham, a pure and chaste soul was shot to hell.

It was during that time when my current cadre of "friends" had taken to calling me "Chopper." No one would tell me why until I threatened to beat the breath out of Frank Harrison again. He said, "Rachel told everyone you have a little pecker."

I can't make this up! No wonder I got into fights. I had to defend my "little pecker."

Here's how that all came about. Where do I begin?

In the span of one summer, the one between sixth and seventh grade when I learned I was adopted, unbeknownst to me, the luminous and carefree days of French kisses on the Riviera of my childhood turned into a rocky shore with very little light (unless I consider the blacklight in Pam's basement).

As it was, I was one of five boys, Harry included, in the exclusive club that got to kiss Rachel and Pam. But during that dread summer when everything changed and nothing changed, unbeknownst to me, Rachel, and a few of the boys, those within walking distance of Pam's house, took to meeting in Pam's basement. Shortly after the beginning of seventh grade, that club would occasionally meet in Pam's basement for about 45 minutes before school. Pam lived two blocks from school, and I have no idea where her parents were. I never saw them.

Since I rode the early bus that dropped kids off on the playground before mass each school day, I was able to skip mass and sneak away with Harry one morning when he asked me along to go hang out at Pam's house. No nuns, no teachers, no parent volunteer to monitor the playground and shepherd wayward lambs back into the fold in those days.

Great times…not. One way to describe the feeling I had in skipping mass and going to Pam's is climbing the ladder to the high dive at the public pool for the first time because all my friends had done it, walking to the end of the board, looking down with that queasy feeling in my stomach, and knowing the only way off is to jump. I puffed on pilfered cigarettes. Listened to music I didn't like. I was too weak to say no to a puff of marijuana. Kissing with the occasional offering of a breast beneath a white blouse was great but were Harry and Mitch letting Rachel and Pam put their hand down their pants? And vice versa? I wondered. Occasionally, Pam's older sister, Kathy, who for whatever reason did not attend the Catholic school, offered up her lips and breasts to whomever she deemed worthy that given morning. This was as close as I've ever been to an opium den; no natural light, two sofas around a coffee table, blacklights, smoke.

It was all fun and games until the morning Pam told me to go upstairs to her room where Rachel was waiting. (Did Pam even have parents?) It's quite probable that in middle school I had fantasized about being in a girl's bedroom. At the very least, I must have tried to imagine what Rachel or Pam's private sanctum was like.

I walked up those two flights of stairs, from the basement to the second story bedroom, like Judas to Gethsemane, feeling like I was about to betray something I couldn't put my…finger on? Take this cup away from me! When I got to Pam's room, I discovered that Rachel was naked under the covers of the bed. She said I should take off my clothes and come under the covers with her. I was terrified! But what else could I do? Go back downstairs and be humiliated? Go to school and hide somewhere until mass let out and be humiliated when the bell rang? Or comply, which I did. I lay there in terror without an erection or a clue what to do and was humiliated with the name of "Chopper" for the next few weeks.

Rachel got dressed under the covers and left me alone and naked in Pam's bed. Can you imagine? Looking back, I don't know whether to be in awe or in stitches. I got dressed, skipped the basement, and walked slowly to school.

In a footnote to this story, I now reside three blocks from Pam's old house. When our sons moved away, Katie and I downsized into a ranch home in the shadow of St. Theresa's School and I drive by Pam's house at least three times a week on my way to the gym where I work out. It's smaller than I remembered.

⁂

I should say that, in a way, Sister Donna was right. For those two years I didn't really have any close friends. I had aged out of the neighborhood games. Harry was the only kid near home in my grade that attended the Catholic school, and we were drifting apart. And, as far as I knew, I was the only kid at St. Theresa's School that was adopted; I envied them all for it. Playing basketball on the seventh and eighth grade teams was a welcome respite and outlet that might have offered clues to how to escape my demons if I was paying attention. I was a starter, but the season only lasted about seven weeks.

The Angry Years might be best summed up by the story of how the hole appeared in a wall in the bathroom down the hall from my bedroom. From the outlet in that bathroom, the cord for the vacuum could reach most of the upstairs and down the stairs to the main floor. Trouble was that the cord frequently wiggled loose and shut down the vacuum. One day, frustrated by repeated trips to the outlet to wiggle the prongs back in place, I punched a hole in the wall between the outlet and towel bar in the shape of a fist. Many years later, when I heard the Jackson Browne song "In the Shape of a Heart," I thought of this incident.

It was weeks later when my mom found the hole behind a towel I had strategically hidden it behind; we rarely used those "towels for show."

Mom asked me what happened. I explained that I lost my temper because of the vacuum cord. She seemed to understand, for she was aware of my temper due to the condition of the large garment moving boxes in the basement with other fist-sized holes in them. (I got in more trouble for damaging the boxes!) Mom covered the hole in the wall with a flower sticker that barely matched the paint color. Neither my mom nor dad were the DIY type but choosing a sticker over getting the hole repaired properly says something about how they dealt with my anger. In fairness, my dad might have never known that hole existed.

I suppose that's what I did to my own wall, stuck a "dutiful son" sticker over the hole that my adoption story had punched through my beingness for two years, when every weekend I did all my chores: vacuumed, cleaned bathrooms, scrubbed toilets, shook the rugs, swept and washed the floors. I mowed the lawn. Raked leaves and trimmed hedges when asked and shoveled the driveway when it snowed. I cleaned all the windows, inside and out, with Windex and paper towels, twice a year.

(My sisters rarely "lifted a finger" as mom would say.) I remained an altar boy, my prayer card and rosary still within reach on my bedside table.

Mom continued to bake fresh bread and make my lunches and cook delicious dinners every night. My mom had my back through every downfall of my life, since kindergarten when I inadvertently upended a table of hollowed out eggs earmarked for the teacher's Easter egg coloring project, and good grief had that kindergarten teacher ever heard of HARD-boiled eggs? My mom had to blow out the contents of another dozen eggs, through pin holes, for school the next day.

My dad? He just continued to provide for all of us in a way that I only came to fully appreciate some twenty years later. What a man!

You know that question that sometimes gets asked at dinner parties, pubs and on Facebook memes: Would you rather go back to grade school knowing everything you know now, or be given ten million dollars? Hell, I'd take ten cents! I love my life. I cherish everything that happened to me, good and bad. I harbor no ill will, and I am who I am today for all of it.

I'm like that tree which, by the way, still stands and towers over the house on the street behind my childhood home. Is there a finer metaphor for the life of a woman or a man than the rings of a tree? Every outline a year. Some circles wide with grace and receiving, others narrow from pain and misgiving. All there below the surface. Sustaining. How thick is the skin? How rough or smooth? Is there fruit on the branch? What hangs there, a tire swing or a rope?

4
This Is My River

Yesterday I had coffee with an old college teammate at a locally owned cafe called Zanzibar's, a fantastic place where they roast their own beans that they source from all over the coffee-growing world. We weren't close in our playing days; we butted heads nearly every practice. We only reconnected at a gym some twenty years later, after my wife and I moved back home to raise our two boys. We meet about once a month, the banter predictable in the beginning: health updates, check in on the sons and wives. He likes to revisit the glory days of the gridiron a little more than I, probably because his days were more glorious.

The news which I was eager to share, once the pleasantries were exchanged, was going to be a bit of a reveal.

"So, 21, guess what I learned after 49 years of wondering and imagining and believing I'd never know?"

Most of the time we addressed each other by our old jersey numbers. He was 21, a defensive back, and I was 88, a tight end. He being a defensive player, I wasn't sure if he could subtract 49 from 60 so I helped him out. I mean, the smoke coming out of his ears could steam milk, roast beans, and set off fire alarms.

I threw him a line, "I was eleven when I learned I was adopted."

I thought he would say something like, "Dang, 88. You must have been one fugly looking child for your momma to give you up." (Once a d-back, always a d-back. Never pass up a chance to trash talk.)

I really hoped he would say something like, "Dude, what took them so long to tell ya?"

But all he said was, "I didn't know you were adopted."

"Yeah. It just never came up. I mean, why would it? Anyway, so yeah, I was adopted as an infant and my mom and dad didn't tell me until I was eleven."

I went on to state the belief I've held my entire adult life, that parents should tell their child about their adoption as early as age four or five.

His response was both funny and unexpected. He said, "I think your parents got it right. What's little junior gonna do, go to preschool the next day and run around saying, 'I was adopted! I was adopted!' or be like, 'Daddy, did you pick me out of a shelter like we got Buttons?'"

To which I replied, maybe a little defensively, "You're wrong!" Just kidding. I went on to explain that I really think the conversation should begin as soon as the child can understand terms like "We love you," and "We chose you," and "You're the greatest gift we've ever been given," and "You belong here," as long as the parents are willing to continue the dialogue as openly, often and deeply as the child needs, for years to come, through all the various questions and levels of understanding.

At that point, 21 revealed, "My ex and I gave up a baby for adoption when she got pregnant a few months before our divorce."

I listened to his story with great interest as I finished my coffee and I realized I wasn't going to get to MY big reveal, that I had recently learned the identity of my birth mother, because the coffee had knocked on the proverbial knee of my gastrocolic reflex with a 22-ounce framing hammer and I had just enough time to get the kids to the porcelain pool at home if I left in the next three minutes.

To which 21 replied, "What?"

"I gotta take the kids to the pool."

"Your boys are in Oregon and California."

"Dude. I gotta take a dump and I'd rather do it at home."

"Ahh. Gotcha."

I told you he was a d-back; he tackled with his head far too many times. Anyway, we departed the cafe with the required urgency and I pulled into my garage at home just as the "kids" were kicking off their flip-flops.

Would you believe me if I told you that my old creative writing professor, Eunita B. Reiten, once told me that memoirs are like baby showers and there can only be one reveal per chapter? No? Dear reader, I'm eager to tell you about Rita, my birth mother. May I prevail upon your patience for a time? I hope to make the wait worthwhile. I waited 49 years.

The conversation at the cafe with 21 got me thinking. Was he right? Did my mom and dad do well by waiting to tell me at the age of eleven?

I've concluded that maybe it isn't so much when parents tell a child, but how. When a child learns he or she is adopted, they should come away feeling like the most special and cared for kid in the world. That their story is as amazing as it is common.

I would take my child to a special place; a beautiful stretch of river comes to mind. A place where a small creek or stream joins seamlessly where the river bends without a hint of turbulence. A place worthy of a ritual.

First, we'd talk about what we see; a strong current, the abundance of life in and around the flow, the beauty of the confluence and how it makes a river stronger downstream and adds such richness beneath the surface. We'd talk about the source of the two rivers and the presence of those sacred waters where we stand at that moment in time. We'd wonder at the mystery of what flows beyond the horizon.

We'd talk about how one's life is like a river, with parallels and meanderings, floods and droughts, stillness, and rapids and falls, all the influences and confluences.

Only then would we talk of adoption. Of how in my case, as an infant adoption came at the source, where snows melt at the Continental Divide or artesian wells spring forth upon the Great Plains. We'd speak of beautiful and pure beginnings that have led to this moment of knowledge, this confluence, this day of revelation.

That is how I would tell my child, at age four or eight or eleven.

And yet, for all of that, I can honestly say that I hold no ill feelings towards my mom and dad for the way they told me. With age comes wisdom, gratitude and the grace that comes with understanding and forgiveness. They did their best.

My dad was the quintessential man of few words. The oldest of eight kids who came of age in the Great Depression. An army veteran of WWII who served in a medical unit in the Pacific, and what horrors he must have seen but would or could never express. A man who worked six days a week and worried for seven while providing for three kids and a wife, and a dog he tolerated. A man who despised leftovers, who wanted nothing more at the end of the day than a couple of Jim Beam's on the rocks and his favorite chair. He had no hobbies, unless watching his beloved Cubs on WGN was a hobby, so he worked until the day he died, on a July Monday morning. After filling up his car for the day's sales calls, he returned to the home where he'd recently paid off the 30-year mortgage. Not feeling well, he asked my mom for a glass of water, sat down in his favorite chair, and died of a heart attack, 62 days shy of 74.

My dad was no more capable of making a ritual out of his son's adoption story than the sun can make poetry out of a sunrise. But he is one of the heroes of my story. The source of my warmth. The man who gave me the freedom to say things he could not.

It's more complicated with my mom.

5
Uncle Sean

My mom, the woman who made a ritual out of her kid's trips to the dentist. The dentist! Shirt with a collar. Pants, not shorts. Dresses for my sisters. School shoes. Brush teeth and gargle before going out the door. If you are of a certain age, you likely gargled with that eponymous brown backwater from Baron Lister's laundry on sock day, which will invariably lead you to that mystifying day much later in life, perhaps while writing a memoir, when you realize that your parents chose to purchase Listerine mouthwash over fresh, minty Scope. But I digress.

Mom rounded out the dentist ritual by giving the front seat to the kid with the fewest cavities and allowing the victor to select which ice cream store to stop at on the way home, Baskin-Robbins or Dairy Queen. Sweet!

Kind of a bittersweet reward. The image I had of my mouth when I left the dentist in those days was akin to how my soul felt after confession, clean and pure. So, to me, going for ice cream seemed a bit counter intuitive, like walking out of church and running the willie up the tetherball pole while screaming, "God damn! God damn!"

"Shouldn't we be going for an apple?" I might have asked my mom, if I wasn't certain I had the best set of choppers of anyone I knew.

And I did! How my sisters must have dreaded hearing me tell our dad at the dinner table twice a year for, I don't know, twelve years, that I didn't have ANY cavities. Again!

I'm the only kid I knew who never had a cavity. It was easy to tell in those days because the fillings were dark and easy to spot when a kid yawned or laughed, or if I just simply asked, "Have you ever had a cavity?"

I think it's fair to say that I was a little OCD when it came to my teeth. There were a few years during my youth where I wouldn't eat Oreos or brownies or fudge or chocolate cake because the residue left behind in the pits of my molars looked like fillings, and I thought that is how cavities originated.

Deep down, there's a part of me that believes I've still never had a cavity. That the big city dentist I went to in my mid-twenties, after a few years hiatus, was lying when he spoke to me the words I had never heard spoken, "You have a cavity."

What was I going to say? "You're lying through my teeth, buster. No Ernest Shackleton of a dentist is going to plant his flag on my molar cap!"

Rather, I'm sure I said something like, "Damn. Are you sure?"

He was. Well, it was a good run.

But back to my mom, and rituals. The mystery for me to this day has always been this: how could this mom of mine, herself with the heart of a poet, who could make taking a loaf of homemade bread out of the oven and offering a thick warm slice slathered in butter to her son seem like it was a gift from the gods (which it was), how could she so utterly swing and miss when it came to telling her son that he was adopted?

A great clue towards solving that mystery came to me when I was in my late forties, after my mom had passed away. I'll share it here now.

My mom's older brother, Straten, got a young woman pregnant when he was nineteen. That woman had a baby, who was immediately adopted by Straten's parents in June 1943. By the time this newborn, Sean, became my mom's younger brother in the home, Straten and his brothers were serving in WWII.

There was nothing remarkable about an older couple adopting a baby in 1943. There was no shortage of babies needing stable, Christian homes. The war gave an escape to many fathers unwilling to step up and take responsibility for a life they helped create, leaving thousands of young women few choices: keep the child and brave a world that frowned on single mothers; keep the child and diminish the chance to find a husband or pursue a dream; find a family member to raise the child; or give the child up for adoption.

My grandparents had the means and the devotion. They welcomed baby Sean as if he was their own.

What is remarkable is the vow that was made in the days or weeks leading up to, or just after, the adoption being official. Remarkable, or just plain flippin' weird.

My grandparents made my mom and her three older brothers promise to never tell Sean he was adopted. Never tell anyone! To never bring it up again. Weird, right? It gets weirder.

They did it! They kept it a secret from my Uncle Sean until every one of them was dead and gone. And none of my cousins knew. My sisters and I never knew.

My Uncle Sean only learned the truth one day in his sixties when he was applying for a U.S. Passport in

Illinois where he was born, and there was an issue with his birth certificate. He learned at that moment that he was adopted. And since the adoption records were open and available to adoptees in Illinois, Uncle Sean quickly learned that his biological father was actually his youngest older brother.

I was gobsmacked the day Uncle Sean told me the story over coffee at my kitchen table. He reveled in all the details, how his older brother was in fact his biological father, and his parents his grandparents.

Uncle Sean quickly tracked down his birth mother in Florida and learned that his "brother" had gotten her pregnant in high school, and arrangements were made with the girl's family to adopt the child and keep it in the family. Uncle Sean remembered how it was his brother who bought him his first bicycle and taught him to ride, and how he took the time to teach Sean baseball and would often throw the ball with him and his pals.

Uncle Sean recalled to me how he was at his brother/biological father's bedside at hospice in the days leading up to his death from cancer, and the man never said a word about his parentage.

All this is to reveal, then wonder, what a sacred or screwy opinion my mom and her immediate family must have had toward adoption. Toward birth outside of marriage. Toward family honor. Toward protecting your own. Toward embarrassment and shame over an unholy pregnancy.

My mom had passed away a few years before Uncle Sean told me the story of his adoption, so I was unable to talk to her about it. I can only wonder if her attitudes about adoption were shaped by her own younger brother's origins, and the subsequent years spent hiding the truth. Of course, at some point, it wasn't her place to say anything to my Uncle Sean, but damn, she sure could keep a secret. I will say that for her.

Sean got a lot of pleasure out of telling several of his nieces and nephews that he was their half-brother. He never married, died a multi-millionaire, and left all his money to the Catholic high school he attended for his senior year after moving from Chicago with my grandma to live with my mom and dad in Des Moines.

6
The Con Before the Storm

I'm heading into high school. In an alternate universe, this could be the place where I found baseball the perfect outlet for all my restlessness and aggression. How the tight knit brotherhood of my teammates grounded me and eased my longing. How I approached every at bat as if it offered me an opportunity to reach the only home I fully understood. And, of course, how all those years of throwing snowballs had turned me into the most feared and effective pitcher in the state.

Or I might be writing of a fourteen-year-old boy who found a way to channel all his energy and longing into learning the guitar, who found his home in the instrument he mastered and the musical misfits he played and sang with.

Both of those scenarios would have brought me more joy at the time, this I know. What I don't know is where either of those two paths would have led me. And since I happen to love where I am in my life right now, it would be foolish to have regrets. I really don't wish I knew then what I know now, and it is a great blessing to be able to say that.

Some kids know what they want to be when they are fourteen. I often envied that kind of self-awareness. I wasn't that kid. I couldn't make freshman year decisions, let alone life decisions. Learning I was adopted the way I did derailed me; it set me adrift. The only things grounding me were school and, ironically, my family.

And so it was that this leaf of a kid drifted into freshman orientation at Dowling High School in the summer of 1975. There to greet every boy, like a Marine Corps recruiter, was the freshman football coach.

Now, the varsity football team at DHS was a perennial state championship contender, so the freshman football team seemed like a good tree to attach myself to. For me, it promised instant credibility and camaraderie. Roughly half of the incoming boys must have felt the same, because close to one hundred boys showed up for the first practice in August. Probably twenty quit after the first day of two-a-day drills, and by the first game we had a roster of roughly sixty boys.

Football was hard! It kicked my ass! It consumed all my pent-up energy and angst. It chased away the bully in me before classes even started and I didn't get in trouble with my teachers. It rooted me to a point where I could at least be myself, and not be so needful of the kinds of friends that put me off balance. I was a part of something, a team, and because of that, I wasn't so caught up in myself.

My adoption went to the outskirts of my mental landscape during my high school years. It came up in random ways, like a visit to a friend's house where family photos on the wall clearly pointed to a common bloodline. I had a friend who asked me on more than one occasion, when talking about a fellow classmate, "Did you know he/she was adopted?" He asked it in a way that invoked scandal, not pride or wonder. I'd just say, "No, I didn't know that." I never thought to ask him, "Why, what difference does it make?" The question just struck me as odd, and not just a little bit prejudiced.

But the prejudice lived in my own mind, so I didn't hold it against him. By the time I made it to high school, and all throughout, pride was not an emotion that surfaced when I contemplated my adoption.

I had enormous gratitude for where I was; I loved my mom and dad dearly. I could go about my days with the amazing freedom and joy that comes when one knows that they are loved unconditionally. I was mature enough and had enough understanding of my mom and dad's feelings about family, to not feel ashamed. And yet, I never told anyone in high school that I was adopted. Even though there must have been a fair number of adoptees in my class of 400, I still didn't know of anyone like me that I could talk to.

7
Dear Freda

I faked my way through football for nine years; four in high school and five in college. I never felt at home on a football field, often dreaded practice, didn't particularly care for the contact, wasn't highly competitive and probably only had above average athletic ability. I think the only thing elite about me was my ability to outwork others, catch a ball, and execute an assignment for about five seconds at a time. A guy can be a pretender and get away with it in football. At least he could in the late seventies and early eighties. I know, I did it.

There's a reason I didn't wrestle, for example. The wrestling coach knew what I was (not tough enough) and didn't bother to ask me to even try out after the mandatory wrestling unit in P.E. that he taught early freshman year. Pound for pound, wrestlers are the fiercest, most competitive athletes I've witnessed. That wasn't me. I played basketball for a season but I didn't like the vibe. I swam for a season because one of my best friends, Dan deRegnier, was on the team. I played golf for a season because I had a crush on a girl golfer named Stephanie. I ran track my senior year to get my forty-yard dash time down. Football was the only sport I stuck with.

The first game I started at Drake University was the sixth game of the season, a non-conference road game against the University of Colorado at Boulder, a Big 8 Conference school at the time. We won the game and I graded out 100% after my position coach watched the film. I was a true sophomore. I tell you this because I am going to write about how my football career began.

Freshman year in high school. I'm way down on the roster at the defensive end position. The only action I see in games is in the fourth quarter if the outcome is secure. I'm not even on special teams. This pattern would repeat until my senior season. Anyway, freshman year we had a practice, mid-season, the field worn down to dirt between the hash marks. It had rained a bit that day so the field was wet but playable. By the end of practice, I had seen so little action that my uniform was spotless. It was embarrassing! And so, at the end of practice when coach blew his whistle for us to gather, while we all ran from various places on the field to wherever he was standing, I "accidentally" fell to get my uniform dirty so it would not be too obvious to anyone who noticed that I hadn't done shit that day.

As I write this, I am literally going to my Spotify app and typing in Jackson Browne's "The Pretender." I mean, seriously, what in the hell was I doing out there? I wasn't getting attention from girls. None of my closest friends were on the team. There was little reward for the physical demands the coaches put us through, the drills and conditioning routines that sent so many of the other guys to puking under the shade tree beside the practice field. What kept me playing football? Why didn't I play baseball? Those two questions have baffled me for decades.

When I learned I was adopted, I stopped playing organized baseball. At the time, my dad said it was because we couldn't afford it, and I held it against him for years. But really, if that was the reason, and I wanted it so badly, I could have paid my way with my lawn mowing money.

I don't blame my dad anymore. I really believe I stopped making choices for myself. I don't think I understood that I had options. And, I don't know, I'm not a psychologist, but I must have felt at some level that I didn't deserve to play the game that made me feel the most at home, the game that I loved! When I was a kid, I was depressed if a baseball practice got rained out, let alone a game. I started every game I ever played, either outfield, third base or pitcher. I played without fear, with confidence, and I was good. Of all the objects that have come and gone in my life, I still have my first baseball glove; it is my oldest possession.

Oh, I had a ton of fun playing football as a kid in the neighborhood, and on the playground in grade school. We played for hours at a time a few streets away from where I lived, where two adjacent vacant lots felt like Lambeau Field. Flat and treeless, it was perfect! But that joy didn't follow me to high school football.

Fast forward to junior year. No one worked harder than I in practice. I busted my ass on the scout team. I was now a split end/tight end who could run stride for stride with the senior starting tailback in wind sprints after practice every day. All that work resulted in zero playing time, zilch, nada. I didn't even suit up for home games. Home games! Yes, we had a large roster, but come on, who doesn't suit up for home games? Guys that suck, I guess. I vividly remember that humbling fact because I got in a car accident the night of our homecoming game my junior year.

During the summer before senior year, I often ran 12 miles a day carrying either a football or two five-pound weights. I attended Iowa State's football camp. I worked out with the heir apparent starting quarterback. I lifted weights.

The work paid off. I ended up starting every game my senior year. For the first time, I played meaningful minutes in games. But I dropped the first ball that was ever thrown to me in the end zone (I was wide open) because I thought I was going to get "lit up" by an imagined cornerback. That was embarrassing, and one of the telltale signs of The Pretender. The only touchdown I scored that season was a fumble recovery in the end zone. But I blocked well and caught everything else that was thrown to me that touched my hands. At season's end, after the team's failing to make the state playoffs for only the second time in school history, I was named Honorable Mention on the All-Conference team.

Up to now, I haven't mentioned the one thing I did in high school that I loved, which, by the grace of some whim or supernatural visit in my sleep, I decided to pursue on my own. No coach to lure me, no teacher that guided me. I took it upon myself to try out for the fall musical my junior year.

I'd never heard of "Annie Get Your Gun." I barely knew what a theater audition was, let alone what it took to get a part. Of course, I was playing football, a fall sport, so I likely wasn't sure if auditioning was even a good idea, with practices and play rehearsals probably overlapping at best. But I must have known it was a safe path, since auditions were a few weeks into the school year and, by then, it was a well-established fact that I wasn't lighting it up on the gridiron.

I remember going to the local library and finding a recording of the Broadway production of "Annie Get Your Gun." I checked it out and became familiar with the music at home, so I'd be ready for the audition. I had to sing part of a song from the score with the provided accompanist and had to read some scenes, all in front of the director. But what I remember the most was the absolute thrill at seeing my name on the cast list outside the drama teacher's classroom! That drama teacher's name was Freda Nahas.

I reckon I set the stage on fire! I must have! I knocked my audition out of the park! I landed a speaking role, Foster Wilson, with an opportunity to sing in a duet with the leading lady! And how many exclamation points can one use in a paragraph?

It's clear, I loved everything about theater. The audition, the rehearsals, the performances, being backstage in the wings waiting for an entrance, the "theater people". Theater for me was a completely safe place, where everyone encouraged each other, and no teammate threw my cleats in the toilet (as happened during two-a-day practices my junior year, courtesy of a senior linebacker that would end up getting kicked off the team a few weeks later for spray painting an opponent's school after a loss). I could lose myself in a character. What could be more natural for a natural born pretender than to find utter joy in something called a play?

I found success in theater because I intuitively understood how much discipline played a role in being a "natural" on stage. I knew that's what it took as an athlete, even if I hadn't experienced any success to date in sports. I immediately discovered that as long as I did the work and was prepared, I never got nervous, even though speaking in front of an audience would terrify me. Also, I found comfort in the knowledge that it wasn't me up there on stage, I was someone else! I was playing! That was so liberating. (This is a trick we actors play with ourselves: to pretend it isn't us on stage, to hide behind the character we're playing even though we are drawing on what are often our most personal and vulnerable parts.)

And so it was that I discovered another outlet for my fire: acting. There was a fire in my belly in those days. Up until that first play, working out for football was all I had that fed the beast. Now I had the theater, and I knew that if I worked at it like I did football, I could be very good. That's what Ms. Nahas told me.

It's no joke to say that in that one experience, I understood what I wanted to do for the rest of my life. I had everything I needed to be great at something. I had, in abundance, an innate ability to play and create, and an athlete's discipline to care for the only instruments I'd ever need, my body and my voice.

Oh, I should add that theater had a great tradition at my high school. That's what the other cast members kept telling me during rehearsals. I was like, "Okay. I get that. So does football." No, apparently, the theater "tradition" was different. But how? No one would tell me, the newest and greenest "theater person." I only found out at the cast party on the evening of the weekend performance at one of the cast member's houses.

This was the tradition: At some point during the cast party, the lights would go out in the basement, and guys and gals could kiss whomever they wanted.

Unbelievable! This had to be the best kept secret in the school, otherwise everyone would try out for the fall musical. But it was true! I experienced it. Sure, it was doubtful the senior girl playing Annie Oakley would let a freshman chorus member kiss her, but I don't recall being refused by anyone, nor refusing anyone for that matter. I fell in love with theater people! It was the best of times. All of it.

I tried out for the spring play and was cast in that as well. The director of that play, a priest who a couple years later quit the priesthood, told me how well I'd done and how I commanded the stage with great energy and presence. That was cool. Sadly, there was no "tradition" with the non-musicals because the casts were much smaller in number.

So, even though I was starting on the varsity football team, I auditioned for the fall musical my senior year. I think Ms. Nahas understood that I wouldn't be as available for rehearsals as I was the previous year, but she didn't want to not cast me. I think that she saw something she recognized in me, passion.

Ms. Nahas was involved with a local theater company, had been a theater person her whole life, and she was a superb teacher. Many years later she would come to Chicago with her niece to see me play the lead in a play with the American Blues Theater. But that senior year, I got a part in the chorus of "My Fair Lady" where my only line was, "Taxi!" The theater hook was now firmly set in my heart, and thank the gods it was a patient fisherman who held the line.

In case you're wondering, there was "tradition" for the "My Fair Lady" cast party as well. But as a sad footnote, some forty years later, when the son of a friend of mine performed in a musical at the very same high school, he knew nothing of that tradition when I talked to him after the run of his show. Poor kid.

Ms. Freda Nahas died in 1996 at the age of 83. She's a charter member of my personal Hall of Fame and this is my bronze statue in her honor. She is immortal as long as I'm alive. And teachers, if you're looking for some motivation to get yourself going, remember that every day you go to work you have a chance to make a kid feel amazing and, if you're like Freda, they'll cherish you for the rest of their life.

❧

This feels like a nice time to introduce my future wife to this story. Wouldn't it be amazing if I were to tell you that we were in a play together my junior year and had our first kiss during the cast party's "tradition?" Well, no such twist of fate occurred. She didn't do theater. As a matter of fact, she dated the starting running back, the one that I mentioned racing at the end of every football practice during wind sprints.

She was in the grade ahead of me. So, for three years we walked the same halls. Probably drank side-by-side a time or two from the same bank of water fountains. Sat back-to-back on occasion in the cafeteria or library. I'd like to think I said hi to her whenever we crossed paths, but I doubt it since she was a year older and beautiful.

Years later, when we finally did meet in Chicago, I of course remembered her; I'd have to have been blind not to have remembered Katie. She, no surprise, did not remember me, and when we looked through a yearbook together shortly after we met, she said, "No wonder I didn't know you. Look how wide your tie is."

In my defense, it was 1977 when that yearbook photo was taken. Who didn't wear wide ties? But alas, it will be another nine plus years before Katie walks into a bar and asks her best friend, "Who is that guy with your brother?" Ah life, what mysteries you hold.

Like the mystery of how, or why I decided to walk on at Drake University, then a lower tier Division I football program. Of the seven or eight guys in my class that could have played Division I football, I was at the bottom of that list based on senior season achievements. Therefore, I can think of two potential forces that led to that strange "decision."

One, after failing to connect with my future bride in high school, the gods of love, knowing she had an affinity for athletes, steered me toward a college where I'd either meet Katie, or meet someone who could lead me to Katie. Since she went to Notre Dame and I wasn't that smart or gifted, the latter would have to be the play.

Two, my brain and body were locked on autopilot. I was still adrift, not making meaningful decisions for my life. In this case, my best friend, Graz, was enrolling at Drake to study pharmacy. What did I do? I told him I'd enroll there, too, and I'd study pharmacy as well! We were best friends! The closest thing I ever had to a brother! Never mind that I got a D in high school advanced chemistry my junior year. I could do this!

What was I doing in advanced chemistry, you ask? That's the same question the teacher asked me when I asked to enroll during registration at the end of sophomore year. You see, I had a huge crush on a girl named Stephanie and had the misfortune of overhearing her sign up for the advanced class. A few minutes later, I approached the second most intimidating teacher in the school, Mr. McPartland (nicknamed "Boom Boom," he also coached the hockey team), and asked if I could take his advanced class. He knew me well enough to try to dissuade me, repeatedly, and finally caved into my desire. I knew I was in trouble when, on the first day of classes my junior year, I walked into the chemistry room and the smartest kids in my school were in there, the valedictorian candidates for chrissakes! We weren't allowed to use calculators like the other chemistry classes. We had to use a slide rule! "What the hell is a slide rule?" is a question I asked myself for the next nine months.

I should back up, just a little. Prior to our deciding to go to pharmacy school at Drake, Graz and I planned to attend Iowa State University and room together. We were accepted and had our dorm assignment. I was going to major in forestry and all was set for us. I also reached out to the head football coach there, Earle Bruce, and asked if I could walk on in the fall. (It was his football camp that I attended the previous summer.) After hearing that I'd be welcome to try out, I set my sights on doing all I could to be ready. I went out for track to get faster and stay in shape. I was a regular in the weight room. I wasn't thinking.

Then, in the spring of senior year, my buddy Graz came up to me, down in the dumps, telling me that his pharmacist dad was making him go to the same school he went to and that his older brother and two older sisters went to, all pharmacists. He couldn't let down the family. Without thinking (are you seeing a pattern here?) I said, "That's all right, man. I'll go with you." And so, I did. I enrolled, was accepted, called the Iowa

State coach to tell him plans changed, then called the coach at Drake, Chuck Shelton, to offer my services as a walk-on. He said I was welcome to join the team in the fall, and we left it at that.

Let me just say here that most college football coaches welcome walk-ons. They have nothing much to lose, and at the very least, will have a warm body to throw into the scout team rotation during practices. Hell, all I had to offer was that I was coming from a high school program that regularly placed athletes in what we now call Power Five conferences. Without that cred behind me, they'd probably have told me to focus on my studies and, "Thanks, but no thanks."

Graduation came and went and about half the summer was gone. I hadn't heard from the football coach since that original conversation probably three months prior, and so my true feelings for the game of football were taking hold. I stopped working out. I figured they forgot about me, and I was okay with that. I was working in a warehouse for my dad's friend, Ray McHenry, who owned a beer distributorship. I bought a car to take to school, a 1969 Mercury Marquis. I had my class schedule. I was all set to be an ordinary student. Then, one day in mid-July the phone rang.

It was the head coach. He was calling to give me all the details of when to report to camp, what dorm the football team stayed at in August while two-a-day practices were happening, what to bring to camp, everything.

Oh no!

"Yes, coach, I'm still planning to be a walk-on on your team…I'll be there, coach…Thank you, coach."

No, no, no!!

I hadn't been working out. Just adrift. What in the hell was I thinking? Within two weeks my urine was brown, and it burned when I took a piss. My stomach ached all the time. I went to a public health clinic to have them test me for an STD and a girl from my high school class was working at the reception desk. I said, "Hi, Staci," got a drink of water and walked out. The symptoms kept on so I went back and, thankfully, she wasn't there. I got the test. They stuck the swab into my penis and that stung like hell. A day or two later they called to tell me the test was negative. No STD. The nurse asked me if I'd been under any stress lately, as that can alter the color of one's urine. Yeah, a little stress. Mystery solved. I don't know how I could have had an STD anyway.

And that is how I became a Division I college football player. Five-star recruit? More like one-star crapshoot.

8
Fine Hearts

I'll wrap up my college football career in one paragraph. Freshman year I had my ass handed to me daily on the scout team by two defensive backs that were drafted into the NFL the following spring and a linebacker named Joel Jones whose forearms were to my body as a Peterbilt on the highway is to a deer. Running opposing team's plays against the starting defense and practicing through at least two concussions made me tougher. Sophomore year I went into the season as the number two tight end on the depth chart. I started the final six games of the season when the starter, an All-American, blew out his knee just before halftime of the Texas Arlington game. In the spring following my sophomore season, I was awarded a full scholarship with room and board included. Junior year I severely sprained my ankle in the final scrimmage of fall camp, one week prior to the first game. I lost the starting job when they moved an All-American wide receiver to tight end and saw limited action during games; that All-American went on to play tight end in the NFL for several seasons. Senior year I was part of a tight end by committee rotation. After that season, I was offered a retroactive redshirt and a fifth season, which I accepted. Not long after, I tore a ligament in my knee during spring practices. My fifth season, after being limited to special teams for the opener, I won back the starting tight end position, yet missed two games mid-season due to a serious viral infection in the repaired knee. My mom and dad attended every home game and several away games. I have one lifetime friend from my football days, Ken "Big Daddy" Tucci, and that is good.

These days, when the topic comes up, I can say with a bit of pride that I played college football at a high level. Not many men can say that. But it was never "play" for me. As I've said, the game never came naturally. For most of my teammates, it really was play; dudes flew around the gridiron like puppies on a beach. Some of those puppies were pit bulls, some were huskies, some were golden retrievers, but they all lived for Saturdays in autumn.

At its best, football is a glorious game. For all the pretense I carried when I donned that uniform to run through the tunnel onto the stadium turf or practice field, to clash with the player across from me, to draw blood and shed blood, I will say without a doubt that football made me a man.

Academically, I dropped out of the pharmacy school after one year and two academic probation semesters. I ended up with a B.A. in Education.

In five years of college, no one knew I was adopted. It just never came up. Does it ever? Thinking about it, I could have gone my whole life without telling anyone. At some point, what difference does it make?

That's the attitude I had in college. I still didn't know anyone that was adopted, and I wasn't close enough to anyone to bring it up, until I met Chrissy.

As I mentioned, I received my diploma in the spring of '84, a deeply committed member of the "five-year plan." What was nice about that extra year of football eligibility was that I had space in my class schedule to take some electives. This gave that old patient fisherman an opportunity to reel in the line and sign me up for a theater class. And so it was that after five autumns of Division I football, I found myself in the basement of the Fine Arts Center on campus in a black box studio theater/classroom and instantly felt more at home than I ever did on a 120-yard-long acre or so of grass.

But that's not to say that I didn't use my previous life on campus to some advantage. Who had ever heard of a football player coming down and taking a theater class? There was an instant mystique around my being there. I felt it. I welcomed it. I also sensed that I'd have about one chance to be taken seriously, and so I better not muck it up.

I was aided in this effort by two facts. One, an acquaintance I made in my first year living in the dormitory and who lived on the same floor, happened to be enrolled in the theater department. He was a freshman when I came into the dorm as a junior, so by the time I came into the theater department in my fifth year, he was an established junior. We immediately became best of friends, and he is the guy who would one day lead me to my wife Katie…but I digress.

In addition, the teacher/director/theater professor of the class I enrolled in was a Pittsburgh sports fan in general, baseball fanatic, World War II veteran and unquestionably the greatest mentor and elder friend I would ever know in my life, Dr. William S.E. Coleman. Or, as he was referred to by all in the department and whom I would affectionately call for the rest of his life, and to this day when I talk about him, "Doc."

The class was called Auditioning 101. Although it may be an exaggeration to say I learned everything I needed to know about acting for the stage in that class, it's not far from the truth. Doc took me under his wing and, in one semester, gave me a master class on acting, because essentially everything one uses to create an amazing audition, he or she can expand upon to create a performance.

I parlayed what I learned from Doc into auditioning for the University's summer professional repertory season and was cast in two of the three plays. It was 1984. I also took a dance class on campus that summer and nearly had a mental breakdown when I realized that while I was getting mauled and maimed in football practices for five years, there was a studio on campus where dudes could leap and stretch with young athletic women in leotards and they'd literally jump into their arms. It was in that mixed state of awe and wonder that I met Chrissy, a dancer in the class.

The following fall, the theater department had some unused scholarship money and basically found a way for me to take enough acting classes so that I'd be eligible to act in productions. I auditioned for Macbeth and was cast in the title role. The 1984-85 school year was theater immersion to the extreme: classes, history, Shakespeare, stagecraft, costuming and make-up, lead roles in three full productions, plus valuable scene work and an invitation to compete in the American College Theater Festival.

I was 6'1" inch tall and could dunk a basketball. Thus, I had the athleticism of a dancer, but none of the moves and little of the balance and control. Dancing in the theater requires…Psych!! You thought I was going to go on and on about dance? Relax. You don't need to skip ahead.

Chrissy is the first gal I ever…courted? I was so painfully shy in high school that I never went to a homecoming dance or prom. I went to two winter formal dances because I was asked. I spent my entire sophomore year agonizing over asking a girl out on a date (remember Stephanie of advanced chemistry fame?), until, faced with the prospect of going an entire summer without seeing her, on the evening of the final day of school, I called her on the phone. It went something like this:

"Hi. Is Stephanie home?" (No cell phones then. When a guy called a girl, he had to risk going through her father.)

"Yes. Just a minute."

Silence.

"Hello?"

"Hi, Stephanie. This is Tom Geraty."

"Hi Tom."

"Hi. Um. Would you like to go out on a date with me?"

"Sure, yeah."

"Um, okay."

Silence.

"Well, I'll, ah, call ya."

"Okay."

"Well, bye."

"Bye."

I never got up the nerve to call her back. She must have thought I was the lamest dork in our class.

I'm going to pull the gentleman card and not go into the lurid details of my several dalliances in college with the opposite sex, other than to say I only had one "relationship," that with the friend of the woman Graz was dating. We went out a lot together, as a couple (them) and their two friends (us). Next thing we knew we were dating; it lasted about two months.

Every other encounter/relationship prior to meeting Chrissy lasted anywhere from one night to a couple weeks. They included such verbs as kiss, fondle, pant, pet, caress, tongue, rub, grind, finger, and stroke. They included the flow of juices but not the exchange, if you know what I mean. You don't know what I mean? Well, okay, I was still a virgin.

The women I might have had serious relationships with in college I put upon so high a pedestal as to make them unobtainable to my shy nature.

Here's an example. I took an astronomy class and there was a woman in that class that was probably the prettiest gal I'd ever known up to that time in my life. As the gods that delight in the torture of young men would have it, we sat beside each other in the lecture hall. We became friends of a sort, studied together sometimes, talked after class, walked to the observatory together. I think she knew I was overwhelmed by her beauty. Anyway, one day I called her at her apartment off campus to see if she was home because I needed to return a book I had borrowed. She was there. I said I was on my way over and I walked the quarter mile to her residence. I knocked on her apartment door and she greeted me, her long brown hair wet, her body wrapped in nothing but a towel. Sometimes when I hear Van Morrison's "In the Afternoon," I think of her and smile at the man I wasn't that day (or was), either too naive or scared or incredulous to walk inside that door. I gave her the book and left. And what is either amazing or simply a page out of the "How to Seduce a College Male" handbook, the exact same scenario played out with an actress in the theater department when I returned a script to her apartment, and she greeted me at the door clad in nothing but a cleavage-exposing robe and her wet blonde curls. Same lame outcome: "Here you are. Gotta go."

I suppose it's fair to say that I courted Chrissy. We lingered after dance class and talked for long stretches of time. She was a couple years younger than I, and she was a theater student at the University of Iowa, living at home for the summer while getting some theater credits at Drake where her dad was dean of the law school. She was adorable and looked amazing in a leotard, but she was unlike any woman I'd ever met; approachable, humble, and kind. (Truth be told, I hadn't completely overcome my shyness. A friend of Chrissy's that I knew from the theater department named Andrea was also in the dance class and I'm certain I did a little reconnaissance work with her before actually asking Chrissy out on a date.) She didn't seem to need anything, and I felt one hundred percent at ease with her. She and I were both strong in our respective Christian faiths, herself a Christian Scientist, something that was important to us back then.

Soon I met her family. I was warmly received by her mom and dad although I had a feeling that having his daughter meet a former football player was not the outcome Chrissy's dad had in mind when she enrolled for a summer dance class. Truth to tell, I couldn't blame him. Let's just say that there were scandals within the football program that involved athlete's behavior towards women, towards property on and around campus, and which had a faction of the faculty and administration wanting to either shut down the program or gut it to a non-scholarship status. I never knew what side of the divide he stood on, but having been a college football player himself at Dartmouth College, it took a while to gain his confidence, for him to see that I wasn't that kind of football player.

Perhaps I did place Chrissy on a tiny little pedestal. One summer evening we took a walk along a dirt road that began not too far from her street. We paused and stood under the stars, the breeze carrying the smell of the day's fresh cut hay from the nearby farm, stars as clear as they could be from the outskirts of a city, crickets chirping, holding hands, myself wanting so much to kiss her. Finally, like a line from a country song, she said, "Are you going to kiss me, or not?"

If my head exploded when Rachel French kissed me in fifth grade, my heart exploded when Chrissy's lips touched mine. It is one of the three kisses that I will remember for the rest of my life, the third being the first one I shared with Katie, my future wife, and if the day ever comes when I can't remember them, I doubt I'll be much interested in living.

The summer of '84 ended. Chrissy and I continued our relationship from a distance, with precious and sexy reunions occurring whenever I could steal away to Iowa City or she came home to Des Moines to see her family and me. During that time, we professed our love for and to each other.

We were together in the summer of '85, back where it all began. I was officially out of school and working as a waiter, saving up money for my move to Chicago to pursue a career in acting.

Yup, acting is something one must pursue.

⁂

As stated, I was on campus for quite a while after my football playing days were over. I went to the games, hung out with the guys I liked. I worked out in the weight room to stay fit, for the body is the instrument of the actor and I wanted mine to be strong. One day, Coach Shelton called me into his office for what would be football's last plea to keep me in its world. Coach had been contacted by the head coach of Graceland College in southern Iowa who was looking for a recommendation to fill a graduate assistant position. Coach asked me. It would be an opportunity to obtain a master's degree while working as an assistant football coach.

By that time, I had my sights set on moving to Chicago. And so, for what feels like the first time in my life, I said no. I don't mean a no to another piece of pizza or beer. I mean no to a serious question and decision about my life.

Was I done drifting? I was in love with a woman and with theater. I had a vision of my immediate future, and I chose the unknown of a big city and a career I heard was ruthless and superficial over the safety and security of getting an advanced degree and a foothold in a game that took care of its own.

I thanked my coach and left football behind me, buoyed by the bliss of being in love.

9
The Unravelling

Look back on your life. Look way, way, way, way back. If you really meditate on it, I imagine that you, like me, can create a thread that stretches from your birth to where you are right now. This thread is so strong, so impactful, that if any element of it is altered, a parent's career choice, your school, a job, a friend, it's most probable that you wouldn't recognize yourself or your life today.

My thread began when my devout Catholic birth mother, Rita, a recent immigrant from Canada via The Netherlands and then a nurse in Philadelphia, became pregnant in October 1960. After being deserted by her grad student fiancé (so one story goes), and likely not wishing to bring shame to her family, she departed five months pregnant to the small Midwestern city of Des Moines, Iowa, to live with a nursing friend who had recently gone home to prepare for an upcoming wedding. They shared an apartment while Rita took a job as a nurse and planned with the local Catholic Charities to find a home for her baby.

That is a profound beginning to a person's thread: mine. Obviously, change anything there and my life becomes unrecognizable. But what about the most random events along that thread? Like the street in the subdivision my mom and dad moved to when I was three years old. Or, to reduce things to their most random, like the route I often ran while training in the summers before football season.

Those very random events led my dad to becoming friends with his neighbor, the beer distributor, where I would later work delivering kegs on occasion to places like The Waveland Tap, which happened to be on the future running route where I passed the owner one day while he was standing out on the sidewalk having a smoke and contemplating both the roster of the pub's softball team and the hiring of a bartender/doorman. I said yes to it all.

Fast forward a couple years to my move to Chicago... you hoped this was leading somewhere.

Chicago seemed like the perfect city for a Midwestern boy to launch an acting career. Los Angeles was unfathomable to me, and New York City loomed too large. My Uncle Dan lived on the north side of Chicago, not far from where he and my dad grew up. Uncle Dan offered me and my theater department friend a place to stay in his basement while we found a suitable apartment for us to share.

As a side note, if the Chicago Symphony Orchestra had a whistling section, my Uncle Dan would have been first chair. My God, it was like living with a canary for that week, until my pal and I took out a year lease on an apartment on the far north side, in Rogers Park, in a building where Dan did some plumbing work. Within a week, my mom and dad arrived with a U-Haul full of furniture to start me off in style.

Before that, Uncle Dan took me aside and told me there was a big hotel downtown on South Michigan Avenue, the Chicago Hilton and Towers, getting ready to reopen after a multi-million-dollar renovation. He thought I should go down and apply for a job. I did. In the section where I had to list previous employers,

I mentioned my gig at The Waveland Tap, handed my application to the HR person and started to walk away.

I got about five steps down the hallway when she called me back.

"It says here that you were a doorman?"

"Yes ma'am."

I didn't feel the need to tell her that "The Wave" was a roughly 600 square foot neighborhood bar that the local rugby club called home, or that my doorman duties included checking IDs and controlling how many folks got in on Thirsty Thursdays when the pub was at capacity.

"Great. We'd like you to take your application down this hall and when you come out on the carpeted lobby, turn left, and see Mr. Carr in his office."

Mr. Carr was the Director of Guest Services and he hired me to be a doorman on the spot. Orientation started in a week.

I worked the 7 a.m. to 3 p.m. shift. I boarded a southbound train at Jarvis, one stop from Howard Street and the northern Chicago city limits, at about 6 a.m., often grabbing a donut and small coffee from the vendor at the station before waving my monthly CTA pass to the lady in the booth. By 3:20 p.m., I was on the northbound train from the last subway stop in the Loop, five days a week, my pocket bulging with cash from the day's tips. Sometimes I needed two pockets! Once a week I walked to the bank with wads of cash hidden under my shirt or coat to make my deposit. All because I had been a doorman at The Waveland Tap.

It was a sweet gig. Thanks for the tip, Uncle Dan! But the work was hard. Michigan Avenue in the winter is no picnic. Working outside in the summer in a long black coat and black top hat is not for the faint of heart.

Riding the El train for an hour-and-a-half six or seven days a week took its toll. I worked at the hotel Wednesday through Sunday, and I used my off days to make the rounds of the talent agencies downtown and do any auditions I could land.

Life was a grind. After the one-year lease expired, I moved into a studio apartment by myself and cut my commute by almost half. That helped, but big city life was eating me up. Another winter was on the horizon, and I dreaded it. Everything that made the city livable to me was about to turn cold: walks along the lake; Wrigley Field; a diverse, character-enriched, half-mile walk to and from the El station each day. To gird myself, I went out and spent over $400 on the biggest, thickest, highest rated parka I could find. With a hood lined in wolf fur and thick with down, I could have put it on without a shirt and stood like a figurehead at the tip of Navy Pier in a January wind and stayed warm.

The thing about working as a doorman at one of the biggest and, at the time, trendiest hotels in Chicago, is you meet a lot of people. People from all over the country would arrive in a taxi, pull up for an event, or need a taxi to a restaurant or convention center. At least once a week, someone would look at the guy opening their door with the warm welcome, me, and say, "You look so familiar," or, "Do you have a brother named such and such?" or, "Is your name such and such?" or, most often, "You have the map of Ireland on your face."

Every time that occurred, I thought of my adoption. It wasn't like this dark cloud came over my face and I got lost in the baggage storage room of misbegotten musings. It simply made me wonder if I had a sibling "out there." And if I looked Irish, then by God I really must be Irish, like my mom and dad had raised me. As a matter of fact, I knew I must be Irish because my best friend in Chicago, Patrick Kelly, was 100% Irish, and his mom and dad said I looked like I just got off the boat.

It was during this time that I adopted Ireland as my motherland, fatherland and holy land. I bought a map of Ireland and taped it to my wall. I discovered where traditional Irish music was being played live in pubs. I had long ago tried Guinness, as it was one of the beers my dad's friend distributed, and I thought it delicious. Hell, there was even an Irish pub called Kitty O'Shea's in the southeast corner of the lobby of the Hilton where I worked! I set about making plans to go to Ireland.

By August of '86 I was becoming physically ill. I landed a small role, the second of my short career, with a relatively new off-Loop theater company, American Blues, on the near north side. Rather than take the El home further north after work, I'd find ways to kill time; I didn't want to go home, only to get back on the train and come back south again to go to the theater. Many times, I'd simply get off the El, walk about a mile to a spot less than a block from the theater, have some food, and lie down in a solitary patch of soft, green grass surrounded by a gas station and a fast-food restaurant, where not two but three major streets intersected: Fullerton, Clybourn and Ashland. I often held a hundred or two small bills in my pockets. It was crazy, and no doubt I was often mistaken for a homeless person. On a few occasions, the director woke me up on his way to rehearsal. During the run of the play, I remember lying curled up in a ball on a sofa backstage because my stomach hurt so much, conserving my strength to go on stage and do my part. I didn't understand what was going on with me. I loved acting, but my stomach was in knots and my spirits were fading fast.

I can recall the weight that left me when I left the city in those days. It was easy to trade shifts with the other doormen, so weekend trips to visit Chrissy in Iowa City or my folks back home became more frequent. No matter where I was with Chrissy, I felt at peace, even when I took her to New York City to see the exhibit of "Van Gogh in Saint-Remy and Auvers" at the Metropolitan Museum of Art. I knew then I would never be an actor in New York, but with Chrissy by my side, the city was lovely.

It was around that time that I asked her to marry me. I don't remember the exact date.

I had asked one of the doormen, a lifelong Chicagoan, where a guy might buy a diamond ring. Also, a lifelong bachelor, he didn't have anything specific to recommend, but he told me about Jewelers Row on South Wabash Avenue. Now that I think of it, I should have asked Uncle Dan. That guy knew Chicago! I know he would have hooked me up. He would have asked all about Chrissy in his blue collar semi-gruff manner. He would have asked if she was Catholic…no. He would have asked where she was…school. He would have asked how we met and if I knew her ring size…in dance class, and yes. He would have asked if I had asked her father…nope.

My dad never told me that it was a gesture of respect to ask the father for his blessing and to give him a chance to rake me over the coals. My dad and I never had "The Talk." The closest we came was the time or two when he took me aside, probably because he noticed his calendar samples had been rifled through and asked me if there was anything I wanted to talk about. Ummmm, no. I didn't know that I was supposed to ask Chrissy's dad for her hand.

I went to Jewelers Row one day in the summer of '86, after my shift at the hotel. I had my checkbook with the five-figure balance, but I didn't let on to the jeweler that I was THAT loaded. I picked out a ½ carat emerald cut diamond and a setting in white gold, picked it up a few days later when it was ready, and took it with me the next time I went home.

Chrissy always came home when I did, unless she was in a play at the University of Iowa. On a summer night that had to have been much like the one when we kissed for the first time, at the same spot as that kiss, I asked her to marry me. She said yes.

Asking Chrissy to marry me seemed like the most natural progression in what felt like the most natural and purest of loves. We didn't talk about setting a date. We didn't talk about the size of the ceremony or any of those details. We probably talked about a honeymoon (who doesn't fantasize about that?) but I don't recall any specifics. The fact was, we both believed we were going to spend the rest of our lives together, so we might as well tell our world. Our parents greeted the news with a fair amount of shock and were relieved that we hadn't set a date. My mom and dad adored Chrissy, but I think they, along with Chrissy's folks, had concerns about our differing religious beliefs. It didn't much matter to us at the time.

As I sit here looking at my notes, where I've sketched out a timeline of the major events of my life, I see that in a little more than twelve months after asking Chrissy to marry me, I was selling her ring back to the jeweler and planning my exodus from Chicago. My head spins a little trying to put my finger on why, other than that it was a very turbulent time in my life and mind.

I quit my job at the hotel in that stretch, in the spring of '87, after enduring a second winter on Michigan Avenue. Mr. Carr tried to talk me out of leaving, but my mind was set and, in those days, an idea in my mind was a hard thing to reverse. Still, I might have stayed with the job had it not been for three things:

One: the varicose veins that emerged around my ankles gave voice to what my feet, ankles and knees were trying to tell me, that standing on cement for eight hours a day in black dress shoes was not doing them any favors. I remember the day I noticed the thin purple lines when I peeled off my black socks in the employee locker room. It was like they appeared overnight. I didn't like that.

Two: I had been cast to do a national voiceover for a fast-food chain's NFL promotion. That was a roughly three-hour job that paid me about $18,000 with residuals ($47,000 in today's dollars).

Three: I auditioned for and won the lead role in a play.

So, with enough money in the bank to support myself easily for a couple years, I quit my job. Ostensibly, I wanted to give 100% of my time and energy to acting. In fact, I was beginning to let go of everything I had and loved. That included Chrissy.

I can see where Chrissy and I are at in our lives today (we have bounced around on the periphery of each other's lives over the years and remain friends). As regards religion, she is very much immersed in Christian Science whereas I am a non-believer, in Catholicism or any religion. I also think our parenting styles and philosophy would have clashed. Which basically says to me that our breakup might have been for the best, and clearly neither would have it any other way today. I consider her one of the two female loves in my life before Katie became THE love of my life.

I know Katie will read these words one day. I trust that she will not feel hurt or threatened by what I'm saying. I trust that Katie knows and understands that what I understood about love in my twenties could be described as me standing amidst a grove of redwood saplings 600 years ago and thinking I knew what world they would become. And that love and life with Katie and our two sons now is akin to calling Redwood National Park my home.

I think it is okay to say I loved Chrissy, and it is okay to say I love her still. For all I know, she helped make it possible to love Katie more fully. A former love is just that: former. But it is a part of a whole, a cherished whole, and I could no more remove those former feelings than I could cut out the inner rings of a tree. We are who we are for all the past glories and pain.

Speaking of the tree rings in the life of a man, the greatest theatrical moment of my life was unfolding…of my life! Nothing ever matched it to this date. That's not to say I haven't had great experiences. But it is almost like I knew in my soul, even then, that what was happening would never come my way again. Thirty-five years later, it remains the fattest, juiciest ring on that branch of my tree called Acting.

It started with the audition. I blew the roof off that storefront theater where American Blues was holding auditions for the only two plays of their '87 season. I was perfect for the lead role in both, so I auditioned for both. I went against what I had been taught about auditioning and prepared a monologue from each play. Conventional thinking was that an actor shouldn't use material from the play being cast, to avoid presenting a vision that might ruffle a director's feathers. I figured, "Fuck it." I'm going to win the role because I'm the best. I'm going to show the director what he has before him and make it impossible for him to see anyone else in the role.

I planned my audition. The first role was for a drifting cowboy-type named Hal who comes to a small Kansas town, rocks everyone's world, then hops a train bound for anywhere but there, in William Inge's "Summer Brave." For that part of the audition, I created a monologue out of a series of lines the character spoke during a particular poignant scene. I wore a patterned western-style shirt with those pearly looking snaps that a guy could just rip off.

The second lead role was for a homeless character, a stoker named Yank, who worked in the bowels of a transatlantic ocean liner shoveling coal into a furnace in Eugene O'Neill's "The Hairy Ape." In my apartment, prior to the audition, I took charcoal and dirtied my torso and arms before I donned the snappy shirt. The transition between monologues was going to be critical, so I practiced until it was flawless.

The directors of both plays were there, as well as some designers and a couple of the theater's founders. I arrived early, for it was ingrained by every coach I ever had that, "If you're early, you're on time. If you're on time, you're late." I awaited my turn. It's possible that an acting mantra that I learned early on in my career was running through my mind while I visualized myself burning down the stage: "Make 'em wanna fuck ya!"

They called me to the stage. I introduced myself, told them that I had prepared two monologues and dove in. After the first piece, I turned my back to them and ripped the shirt off my back. Naked to the waist, I pulled a piece of charcoal out of my pocket to dirty up my face and neck to complete the image and present the fierce bravado of a man who shoveled coal into a stokehole for his living.

The director called me that evening and offered me the role of Yank. We workshopped and rehearsed for a couple months, part of the time in a bomb shelter below street level on West Fullerton Avenue. We got rave reviews, played to sold-out houses, and when people talked about "Chicago Theater," they often cited our production.

People told me that playing Yank in "The Hairy Ape" was the role of a lifetime. Who knew? Nothing I've done since, in 35 years, has touched it. We caught lightning in a bottle.

The director and designers had an incredible and daring vision, and every one of them had the passion and skill to pull it off. The ensemble of actors was the most selfless, committed, trusting, energetic and inspiring I've ever had the sweet joy to work with. The performance space was so intimate that I could touch the knees of those sitting in the first row. There was a thunderstorm in Chicago the night we opened, July 13, 1987, and the building shook as if the Theater Gods were landing on the roof to see what we were doing. Lightning in a bottle.

Later that summer, the chief theater critic for the Chicago Tribune, Richard Christiansen, wrote a feature on the previous season's production and performance highlights. He singled out "The Hairy Ape" as an outstanding example of the gritty, gut-punching style of "Chicago Theater," and he singled out a local actress and me as "actors to cherish, and they are ours."

But I wasn't really. I wasn't "theirs." Part of what made me effective playing the role of Yank was that I related so well to what he was going through. Yank belonged, was at home, in the stokehole of an ocean liner shoveling coal into a furnace, breathtakingly powerful while at work. But on land he was always adrift, struggled to fit in and wondered where he belonged. I knew that guy. I'd been living with him since I was eleven years old.

Don't get me wrong, I was having the time of my life! For example, I don't remember how many times I woke up in the summer of '87 and said to myself, "I think I'll walk over to Wrigley today and see what Andre Dawson, Ryne Sandberg and Greg Maddux are up to." I'd walk up to the window beneath the bleachers, buy a ticket, drink an Old Style or two, and watch a Cubs game.

My best friend and theater pal from Drake, Patrick Kelly, had graduated and was living back in his hometown of Chicago. We got into all kinds of beer-fueled shenanigans, all as harmless as the profanity-laden slurs of the order taker at The Wiener's Circle hot dog stand when we ordered cheese fries at 2 a.m. in those gloriously colorful days before political correctness.

It was during this summer when, if you'll recall, my future wife, Katie, happened into a bar with her best friend from Notre Dame, Colleen Kelly, and asked her if she knew the guy across the bar standing with her brother. "That's Tom Geraty. He's engaged."

I was at that. For about two more months.

By that summer, Chrissy was living in Chicago, sharing an apartment with two other female actor friends, not too far from my studio apartment on Pine Grove.

Tom Waits has a song called "Please Call Me, Baby." There's not a lot in that song that relates to Chrissy and my situation, but there is a line in that song that stopped me in my tracks the first time I heard it, years later while living in Berlin, Germany, and I thought of Chrissy and Katie and acting and everything I thought I'd left behind. The line goes like this: "If I exorcize my devils, well my angels may leave too. When they leave, they're so hard to find."

It never occurred to me to have asked Chrissy if she wanted to wait for me while I exorcized my demons; the restlessness, the wanderlust, the wondering where I fit in. I was becoming desperate to leave Chicago and acting couldn't make the city bearable. Patrick Kelly's mom and dad were like surrogate parents for me. I loved them dearly and they treated me like family. Being in their home was akin to being in another world. But even that wasn't enough. The idea of making a clean break felt like the best way forward for me, and I was fantasizing about getting on a bicycle and riding across the country. With my demons increasing their hold, I took a Greyhound bus home to Des Moines to visit family and friends, got a wild hair, bought a bicycle, and rode like a fiend back to Chicago in three days with my bag strapped to the rear rack. I loved being on the backroads, the solitude, the open spaces.

As I rode back into the city along Highway 64 and North Avenue, I knew I'd be riding out of town in the spring for who knows where. I didn't know when or if I'd ever come back, so the fairest thing I could think to do was end things with Chrissy; and so, I did.

During that time as well, the lease on my studio apartment was up so I moved into a two-bedroom apartment with Patrick. I bought a Rand McNally Road Atlas and began to plot my two-wheeled exodus out of Chicago.

I was also cast in a Shakespeare play, the role of Demetrius, in "A Midsummer Night's Dream." We rehearsed and opened that same spring. I went to the lakeshore with a fellow actress named Catherine Price, who happened to be playing the role of Demetrius' love, Helena. It turned out we weren't acting. While lying on the beach, we looked at each other, smiled, and we kissed. We had a brief relationship, she shared her bed with me, we went to see Dan Fogelberg together. I knew she was a love of my life even then, but I knew where I was going. She seemed to understand, and we parted as friends. And simply because I wish for Catherine to live a bit longer in these pages, I'll mention that I saw her a few years later when I went to visit Patrick after he moved to Los Angeles to pursue a career in cinematography.

Catherine had given up on acting and was in graduate school at Fuller Theological Seminary in Pasadena. Patrick lent me his car and I picked her up on campus.

We had a lovely afternoon, had lunch, and went for a long walk. It was the last time I'd ever see her. Catherine eventually became a Reverend, first in the Kansas City area then finally back in her hometown of Western Springs, Illinois, at First Congregational Church. She never married, except perhaps to her God, and died of cancer in 2008. Dang.

Rest in peace, Catherine Price.

10
The Crucialble

In this story of my life, the moment that the gods of love must have had planned for me since the day I was born, the moment I had been waiting for, really since I was eleven years old, was approaching fast, was now upon me, and I didn't even know it. The love of my life, not a love of my life, THE love of my life, the first woman I would make love with, my heart, my home, my bride, my family, my partner in raising two boys, the woman for whom I would wait with joy and anticipation to hear come home from work for over 25 years as I write these lines, Katie, and I, were about to meet. But first, a little background regarding that day I was born.

My birth mother's name was Rita Petronella Perquin. She was born in Zeist, The Netherlands, in 1934 and emigrated with her parents and three siblings to Canada in 1952. In Montreal, she completed her nursing studies and worked there before the family moved to New York. Eventually, Rita settled in Philadelphia where she worked as a nurse, was engaged to be married, and became pregnant in October 1960, at the age of 26.

Apparently, Rita's fiancé wanted nothing to do with a child, so he left Rita to deal with her pregnancy on her own. It is unclear if any of her family was aware of her situation, since all but her youngest sister, Johanna, was deceased by the time I learned about Rita.

What is known is that Rita left Philadelphia in early March 1961, five months pregnant, to live with a nursing friend that had recently gone home to Des Moines to prepare for an upcoming wedding. The two friends shared an apartment. Rita started a nursing job at Mercy Hospital on March 17 and worked there until a week before I was born, at that same hospital, on Bastille Day. It states in my adoption file that Rita attended mass at the cathedral downtown every Sunday (it's walking distance from the apartment building where she lived) and often in the hospital chapel before or after her shift.

While Rita was working, she began the adoption process with Catholic Charities. (About two years prior to her own pregnancy, Rita cared for her youngest sister, Johanna, through her unwanted pregnancy at 18 and they had a good experience adopting the baby out through Catholic Charities in Florida.) I lived at a place called Christ Child Home from the day Rita and I left the hospital, July 19, until the day I was given to my mom and dad on Tuesday, August 1. Rita, missing her family back east, went home the next day.

It's certain that Rita was not allowed to stay with me until I had a home; it's probably wrong of me to assume she would have wanted to. I don't know how things worked with adoption placements, then or now, or if Rita had a say in where I was placed. It seems reasonable to me that a woman might want to know more than that her baby was going to a safe and stable place. There was no question that my adoptive parents would be Catholic. But maybe Rita, a professional woman of 27, was allowed to choose from a pool of prospective parents, a privilege not normally granted by the powers that be to teen mothers. Who knows? If so, and Rita did indeed have a say, then she left my hometown having bestowed upon me the two greatest gifts of my life, my mom and dad.

I know what else she gave me, my DNA, and the parts of her that any child takes from a birth mother. But I wonder what I gave her before she left. Nineteen days after I was born, Rita left town. Did her hands ache for having held me? Her heart? Did she even get a chance to hold me or was I whisked away to avoid any emotional attachment to foster? Did she shed a tear as my town disappeared from her rearview mirror? Was there a song that played on the radio in that summer of 1961 that forever reminded her of her days carrying me inside her? Did she think of me every year on July 14, maybe take a walk to her favorite bakery and treat herself to something special? Did she think of our time together when my hometown made the news out east? Did she ever tell anyone about me? Was she ever lost in wonder, among a friend or friends, when someone asked, "Rita, where were you just now?"

Rita carried me for nine beautiful months then said goodbye. She never had another child.

It's mostly in hindsight that things seem inevitable. I can sit here now at this keyboard and honestly convince myself that Rita's coming to the Midwest to give birth was part of the plan that had to happen to place Katie and me together. I can make a case that everything that happened in my life from 11:51 a.m. on July 14, 1961, was leading me to Katie.

It was December 1987 when Colleen Kelly and her brother Patrick had their friends, Katie, and me, up to their folks in the Sauganash neighborhood of Chicago's north side for drinks and supper. It was a bit of a holiday party; Patrick's brothers were there, along with some friends of the Kelly's named Larry and Eileen, I recall. Hours of laughter and drinks and great food passed in the blink of an eye. By the end of the night, with all the guests gone, Mike and Trudy Kelly themselves up to bed, all that remained, sitting around a coffee table in the family room to nurse a nightcap and reminisce about the evening, were Colleen, Patrick, and their two friends that just happened to be sitting across from each other. Katie's feet were on the coffee table, clad in black stockings. My feet rested inches from hers, clad in dark dress socks.

Years later, Katie would say it was what her grandpa called "The Atomic Theory of Love." I think there's something to it. No amount of silk, wool, cotton or whatever those socks and stockings were made of was going to stop those atoms from catching fire. I think even had she been wearing ski boots and myself a pair of arctic-rated fishing waders, the sparks would have flown. Amidst sips and laughter, our feet found each other; it was as if they were having a conversation of their own. For about ten minutes, our feet messaged and massaged each other until Katie stood up, took me by the hand to the Kelly's dining room, and surrendered the softest and most kissable lips I will ever know.

In hindsight, 34 years after that kiss, the timing seems so right. The life story that Rita put into motion 26 years prior had met its mate! But in the moment, it seemed like the worst possible time.

I had a road atlas on my dresser opened to the two-page spread of the lower 48 states with a highlighted bicycle route that touched each one. I was leaving Chicago in less than five months! In my mind, I was already gone.

I'd love to have dinner with you.

No, I've never been to O'Fame for pizza.

Well sure, I can come up to your apartment.

Whoa, you have Molson Canadian in your fridge. I'd love one.

Let's sit on your hardwood floor and listen to records.

There's no easy way to get to my place from here on the El.

Let's spend the night together.

That's a lot of pillows.

This is probably the nicest bed I've ever slept in.

That was my first time.

Yes.

26.

It's usually quiet when I write. Sometimes I'll have a little classical music playing low in the background. Then there are times I like to put my Spotify "Liked Songs" playlist on shuffle and see if the music can talk to me, get me kickstarted perhaps, maybe trigger a thought. I currently have 472 songs there, so chances are good that something relevant will pop up. Sometimes, a song will appear that, if this were a movie, would be the only song imaginable to appear in the moment. It just happened when Bob Dylan's "Make You Feel My Love" shuffled in the room. His words are what Katie gave me the night we made love the first time. Play the Adele version if you like for a female's take on this beautiful, beautiful song, and you'll understand that there was no doubt in her mind where I belonged, and yes, I hadn't seen nothin' like her yet.

Inside her apartment, inside her bed, inside her arms, inside her love, inside her, Katie offered me everything I ever wanted and needed in my life. She was a friend and a lover and a home and a woman with whom I could live and create and share a thousand hundred moments and worlds. It's true that I always wanted my first time to be with the woman I married. It happened! She loved me! I loved her! It was as pure and beautiful as I imagined it could be. And I was so tormented, restless, and tied up inside that I left her after five months for a demon that I had to almost die multiple times to kill.

I suppose that's not entirely true. I didn't have to almost die; I just nearly did a few times because of where I put myself in that time I should probably call "The Forsaken Years."

On May 1 I woke up in Katie's bed. She showered and got dressed for her day. We left her apartment together, walked to the corner. We said our farewells as the southbound #11 Lincoln Avenue bus approached. I saw her onto that bus and watched as it headed downtown toward her office. By noon I was riding my bicycle south down Western Avenue. That night I slept in my sleeping bag under the stars beside a golf course fairway somewhere in northwest Indiana; I was back on the road at dawn, headed southeast before the sprinklers turned on.

And Katie? She went on living her beautiful life. She enjoyed her work, had great friends, dated other guys, traveled to Europe and Nepal. We stayed current on each other's comings and goings through our friends, Colleen and Patrick.

11
Camerado and Quixote

These days, Katie will come home from work and ask me how my day was, how the writing is going, how my knees are feeling, etc. Over dinner last night, I told her I had written about our time together leading up to my departure from Chicago and how I termed the ensuing few years as "forsaken". She said, "That sounds so dark and hopeless."

She has a point. I suppose that yesterday I got drawn deep into the fact that I was saying farewell to her and venturing into a life of uncertainty that I now know contained loneliness, pain, depression, and dances with death. It's hard not to get caught up in the mythology of one's life, I guess.

To her point, the fact is, riding out of Chicago was exhilarating. It was the start of the second greatest adventure of my life, the first being marriage and raising a family with Katie.

I named my bicycle Rocinante. I read voraciously while living in Chicago: Hemingway, Steinbeck, Dostoevski, Joyce, Wordsworth, Whitman, and Shakespeare, just to name a few. I read Don Quixote and related to his need to strike out on an adventure and slay some dragons and seek a world that could fit his ideals. It was a no-brainer when, after selling the bike I bought in Des Moines to an actress I did a play with, I purchased a Schwinn Cimarron in early 1988. I began to outfit her and named her after Don Quixote's steed.

My affinity for backroads and small towns and diners was ignited in those sales trips in the summers with my dad when I was a kid. The bike trip was, in many ways, a slow-motion version of those journeys. I planned my day's travels around where I was most likely to find a diner for breakfast about an hour's ride from wherever I slept the night before. For example, I'd look about a hundred miles into my future in the general direction I was headed, and say to myself, "Hmmm. Hillsboro, Ohio, is a county seat, about 6,000 people. They have to have a town square and a diner there." I'd point Rocinante down the highway and start looking for a place to camp around dusk. In the morning, I'd go riding into town a whoopin' and a hollerin' "Blazing Saddles" style, find me that diner, park Rocinante in a place I could keep an eye on her, have breakfast and study my map and drink coffee until nature called, drop a deuce, tip the waitress, and head on down the road.

Once or twice a week, depending on weather or the likelihood of my finding a safe, suitable spot to pitch my one-person tent, I'd snag a motel room. Those were great nights, too. I could stash Rocinante in the room and go sit at a bar, sip a beer, perhaps chat with a local and watch a baseball game. And no, I wasn't "Bike Shorts Wearing Guy," I had a pair of jeans stashed in my saddle bag.

If a town had a public pool that didn't wait for Memorial Day to open, I'd make a stop, cool off and avail myself of their fine shower facilities. Most of the time, however, I "bathed" with baby wipes where I camped. Unscented, of course.

I remember one of my theme songs during this trip was a country music ditty named "Wheels" by a band called Restless Heart. I would sing it at the top of my lungs in the middle of nowhere; I knew every word. No cell phones in those days. I carried no portable music source, no headphones, no radio. Just my voice and the road and the fields and the trees and the wide sky and the horizon. Nothing behind me, everything ahead.

Depending on the wind. Oh, the wind! It could be a blessing or a curse. I remember a north wind so strong one day, myself riding south, that I almost flew down the road. I altered my route that day just to enjoy the feeling of flying. There were days I was riding into a wind so fierce I had to pedal downhill. Merciless! But what I was going to say is that, depending on the direction of the wind, I could smell roadkill either a half mile away or for a half mile after passing it.

I made it across Indiana and Ohio and into West Virginia without a hitch or glitch, unless you count the all-too-frequent flea-bitten, fur-matted, four-or-less legged farm dogs that saw or heard me coming down some otherwise idyllic stretch of serenity waiting to explode out of a bush or ditch to lay fangs to my Achilles, get tangled up in my spokes, or test the contents of my colon for any stubborn turds that missed their cue at the diner that morning. There were times I rode with my tire pump in my hand. I never thought to carry mace, and isn't it refreshing to realize that spellcheck recognizes turd!

To my knowledge, John Denver never rode a bicycle in West Virginia. I'd bet my mom's strawberry rhubarb pie recipe on that. If he had, he'd never have written

"Take Me Home, Country Roads." I can't remember where I entered the state, but I got deep into it before I realized that a guy on a bicycle on narrow winding two lane roads in coal country was about as welcome as a turd on a charcuterie board. (Should I just title this chapter "Turd"?)

I must have entered West Virginia on the weekend when the coal trucks weren't running. Heading in an east-southeast direction, I had it in my mind that I might dip my tire in the Atlantic Ocean somewhere along the North Carolina coast before heading back west. The going was light and breezy at first. Then the roads narrowed, the hills steepened, the trees thickened and grew up to the roadside and the shoulder became little more than the outside lane stripe. I was already on edge when the first coal truck approached, releasing its air brakes, and blasting its horn; I steered off the pavement and stopped to let it pass.

I got back on the road, and five or ten minutes later another truck approached. Keep in mind that these are narrow winding roads of increasing altitude where the absolute last thing a trucker expects or wants to see is a guy on a bicycle.

After, I don't know, five or six of these encounters, I just got off the road until it seemed the trucks were done running for the day. I blazed into the next town and got a room at a motel, licked my wounds, and planned my exit strategy with my companion, Rand McNally.

It seemed to me there was only one way to get out of West Virginia alive, get up at dawn and find the next road west toward Kentucky, ride until I see the first coal truck, pull over for the day, then ride like the blazes from about five o'clock, when the drivers were done for the day, until I came to a town with a motel. There was no place to hide and camp where I felt safe, I had to sleep in motels. I have no recollection how many days it took me to get out of West Virginia. All I know is I wanted nothing to do with the density I believed awaited me further east. I was rattled and I needed wide open roads. I do remember stopping at a bridge that spanned a border river beyond which lie Kentucky. I sat there for a good hour, watching the water, the traffic, and thanked my guardian angels for getting me there alive. I crossed into Kentucky and soon the world opened up again.

If John Denver had ridden a bicycle through West Virginia, his classic song might have gone something like this:

Cycle ridin', West Virginia.
My bike saddle makes my sore ass quiver.
Coal trucks roll there, rollin' through the trees,
Makes me think I should be busking in Belize.

Miner's roads, shoulda known,
Ain't no place I belong. Went to Danville,
Called my mama, so alone,
Miner's roads.

Loaded calories at the diner,
Miner's lady, waitress to this wan'drer.
Pale and busty, "You must be that guy!
Won't you take me with you?" teardrops in her eyes.

Miner's roads, cold as stone,
Rand McNally should have shown, in the legend,

Mountain drama, skulls and bones,
Miner's roads.

I heard a horn in the mornin' hour befall me,
"Cheerio! Remind me why you came this a'way!"
And ridin' down the road I get a feelin'
That I might not see another day, 'nother day.

Miner's road, hold the phone,
I don't really like your tone. Best be seein' ya,
Need a sauna, make me groan,
Miner's road.

There are two towns that I recall riding through in Kentucky, Pikeville and Bowling Green. I remember Pikeville for the relief I felt getting out of West Virginia represented by the tremendous openness and the hill I coasted down coming into town and I remember Bowling Green because it was the biggest city I rode through up to that point after Chicago. I pedaled west into southern Illinois, caught northeast Missouri, a bunch of Iowa (where I stopped at mom and dad's house for a brief respite and some home cooking), and rode about a hundred miles into Nebraska when I just stopped. I put Rocinante and myself on a bus back to Chicago where I still had a share of the apartment with Patrick.

Patrick's brother had a construction company and I worked for him for the next three months. I was paid in cash while learning valuable skills in home rehab, demo, rough carpentry, and finish carpentry mostly. I also hung drywall and did some concrete work.

But I was getting restless again. Some people thrive in the city, they feed off the energy and pace and density. Some people, like me, slowly lose their vitality and peace-of-mind amidst the hustle and traffic and concrete and noise. It's not good or bad, it's just a fact of one's temperament. And so, again, I began to plan my next exodus.

About this time, I learned of a company in Chicago called Auto Driveaway. I made some enquiries and found out that, basically, a person could contract with them to deliver a car for their clients to just about anywhere in the United States. Well, where does a guy want to go that needs healing from big city life, has a longing for adventure and a perpetual yearning for a home he feels he lacks? Why, Alaska, of course.

Unfortunately, Auto Driveaway had no cars that needed to be driven to The Last Frontier. The closest I could get was Portland, Oregon. After bargaining for an extra day, I signed the paperwork and had five days to get to the west coast. I drove through South Dakota and took in the site of the Wounded Knee Massacre, the Badlands, and Mount Rushmore. I paid my respects at the Little Bighorn Battlefield and later sunbathed naked on a boulder atop a mesa in Montana, splayed out like a reptile taking in the heat while meditating on the lands I was seeing that I'd read about in Dee Brown's "Bury My Heart at Wounded Knee." I hit northern Idaho in darkness and drove through the glow and smoke of wildfires. I slept in the car every night. I resumed my love affair with small town diners, road maps and the ingenuity of baby wipes, unaware of how rare it would be to one day arrive at a destination without the aid of GPS or Google Maps. I drove into Portland on an early morning, delivered the car, took in the city for a few hours, rode the train north to Seattle with my backpack, and checked into the YMCA downtown. The next day I explored Pike Place Market, hung out downtown and eventually bought deck passage on the car ferry up the Inside Passage to Haines, Alaska.

    I think that for utterly beautiful and new and awe inspiringly, breathtakingly humbling natural vistas, nothing I've ever experienced matches the nearly two-full-day ferry ride up the Inside Passage. I've been up and down the Irish coast from Kinsale to Donegal town, seen the sun rise and set over Saharan dunes, ridden trains across the Alps and Europe, and felt all types of weather with the Aleutian Chain and the Bering Sea as a backdrop. None of it surpasses the Alaska Marine Highway.

    Deck passage is the least expensive way to gain access to this wonderland of riches. It means one is not entitled to a cabin with a bed and will therefore face the potential harshness of the elements. Once on board, one must hustle to a small portion of a particular deck to set up a tent while the choice spots are free or stake a claim to one of the limited chaise deck chairs with a backpack or sleeping bag. It also means that for less money, one can roll over at night, open an eye and catch a glimpse of what a hundred million stars looks like or a solitary shoreside cabin lit by a single man-made light. Sometimes it must suck ass to be rich.

    I met a guy out on the deck whose name I cannot recall; it was late August 1988 after all. We were both probably sipping beers, standing at a portside railing watching orcas appear and disappear at the surface of the Clarence or some such strait. We had a great chat;

he was moving to Anchorage to start a new job, had his things in a cabin room and his car in the hold. When he learned I was also sailing to the end of the line then hitchhiking the rest of the way to Anchorage, he offered me a ride. I'm pretty sure he drank for free the rest of the way to Haines.

The Alaska Highway and the Tok Cutoff was mostly beautiful and uneventful, except for the did-that-just-happen 360-degree spin out on a patch of gravel that somehow left us upright in the same lane with four inflated tires. Oh, and one very cold night in a sleeping bag. We arrived in Anchorage, probably got a bite to eat and said our farewells. I'd see him again in about 20 months. For now, I was in Alaska and had to figure out what to do.

"The earth still remains free for great souls. Many places–the odour of tranquil seas blowing about them–are still empty for solitaries and solitary couples.

"A free life still remains for great souls. Truely, he who possesses little is so much the less possessed: praised be a moderate poverty!

"Only there…does the man who is not superfluous begin: does the song of the necessary man, the unique and irreplaceable melody, begin."

—From "Thus Spoke Zarathustra," by Friedrich Nietzsche.

I was rooting around my notebooks and random writings from around that time in my life, "The Forsaken Years." I had read that novel by Nietzsche and wrote down that quote. I don't remember much of anything about the book I read, but reading that quote again after so many years, I have a pretty good idea as to why it resonated with me.

Let's see...

Earth remains free and empty for great solitary souls? Check.

Possess little and be less possessed? Check.

To not be superfluous? Check.

To be necessary? Check.

In my supercharged romantic mind, I was all those things! The world was the ripest and fullest of nectarines and I was biting into that bad boy, juice dripping off my chin.

I walked into a construction company's office and got hired on the spot to go work as a laborer up north of the Arctic Circle at Prudhoe Bay where my duties included sucking sludge out of huge empty Arctic Sea saltwater holding tanks with a man that could pass for a monkey because he could go down an extension ladder into the tank and back up again faster than I've ever seen while carrying a hose and yelling, "Shit fire, eat matches." Seriously, that guy, whose name is as unlikely to be found in my memory as an e-car charging station on the North Slope, could go up and down a ladder two rungs at a time in rubber boots like he was running stairs. It was amazing. I drove an eighteen-wheeler flatbed, grinding gears around every turn, over dirt-packed tundra roads to pick up tree-trunk-sized timbers to take back to the site where we built emergency containment pits in case of an oil leak disaster. And yes, I laid on that air horn about a dozen times a trip like a kid hits the bell on a new bike, with nothing to hear me but permafrost and arctic fox.

That gig lasted about two weeks. They flew me back to Anchorage on their chartered plane with a slew of other workers that were cycling out of their rotations. On a wild hair, I rented a car at the airport and drove south down the Kenai Peninsula to Homer because I heard it was beautiful. Oh, yes it was.

Homer didn't get its name from the Greek poet. If the founding miners were going down that road, they'd have dug a little deeper and named the place Circe. I fell under her spell. The afternoon I arrived, I drove the rental car out on the Homer Spit Road and didn't leave until the following morning. I couldn't leave! The sunlight flickering off the gentle waves of Kachemak Bay was mesmerizing and illuminated the mountains rising out of the not-too-distant shore across in a constantly dancing display of seduction to my sense that I'd discovered my newfound home. I called from a payphone there on the spit as dusk approached to tell my mom and dad that I was okay, then rang up my friend Patrick in Chicago to try and put into words where I was. I slept that night in the car.

The next morning, I drove the rental into town, found a great diner and gorged myself, secured a cabin to rent about a mile up the hill/mountain in the pines northeast of town, dropped off my duffle bag, backpack, and groceries, returned the rental at the local airport, took a taxi back to the cabin, settled in and probably said to myself something like, "What just happened?"

The sensible move would have been to tuck this bit of heaven on earth into my back pocket and drive back to Anchorage to find an apartment to rent that had a phone and central heating, maybe a kitchenette, perhaps near a grocery store, a bus route and, I don't know, people. As it was, I was about to get really acquainted with a hot plate and solitude. Neither turned out to be great companions.

I got away from both after about a week. I called the construction company from a payphone in Homer to see if they needed me. They said that if I could get to the Anchorage airport by the next day, I could get on the charter to Kuparuk up on the North Slope near Prudhoe and work as a laborer for a couple weeks with an HVAC contractor. I hauled my ass and my duffle bag to the Homer airport and caught a commuter flight to Anchorage.

In Kuparuk, my companions were a renewable roll of duct tape, a complement of tin snips and a philosopher turned HVAC contractor named Galen whose job was to maintain anything in the vicinity that had to do with air circulation.

It was a good gig, but two weeks later I was back in the cabin. I witnessed my first September snowfall while attending a Homer High School football game and thought, "It's gonna be a long winter."

I've always enjoyed my own company, ever since I was a boy. But tucked up and away at that cabin in the woods with a job that seemed a bit random and required a commute in an airplane, I felt my days in Homer were ending. Add to that the fact that I was lonesome for the Midwest and friends, well, it was an easy progression in my mind to just go home. I packed my bags and did just that.

The nice thing about Alaska is that it really tried to make me feel at home. The beauty, the serendipity, everything was working; I didn't even mention that the man who owned the construction company in Anchorage, and hired me, knew my college head football coach from their days in Missouri. What are the chances of that happening?

But the confounding common denominators through this and all these adventures to date and to come were fierce combatants to idyllic scenery, happy coincidences, and the freedom of carrying everything you own in a large green canvas duffle bag and a backpack or on a bicycle. These inviolable forces had names like Loneliness, Belonging, Restlessness, Homeland, Misfit and Melancholy.

Take Restlessness. One would think that being restless would be satiated by movement and new experiences and places. I was learning that it only got worse the more I moved, but I couldn't help it. I bounced around between Des Moines and Chicago for the next year and a half, sleeping in my folks' basement or on floors or inflatable mattresses in Chicago, framing houses or doing demo or delivering fitness equipment or desk clerking a night shift in a downtown hotel or attending slots in a casino. I took another solo bicycle trip in May of '89, from Chicago through Iowa, Missouri, Kansas, Colorado and New Mexico into Arizona where it reached its furthest point at another "Bury My Heart at Wounded Knee" destination named Canyon de Chelly National Monument. I rode my bicycle in, sat on the canyon's rim with a Native American of the Navajo Nation (I privately imagined he was a distant relation to the great Chief Manuelito), then got a ride out with Rocinante in the back of his pickup. I pedaled back to Santa Fe and met up with Patrick and another great actor friend named Philip Lehl from college. We hung out there for a few days at the home of yet another actor friend named J.D. Garfield. I then put Rocinante in the baggage compartment of a Greyhound bus and rode with the boys back to Chicago.

I knew Loneliness and Belonging couldn't be soothed in the arms of women one didn't love, but I let myself lie with some. Not many. I remember the names of every woman (Mary, Linda, Cathy, Renee, Marilyn, Maria, Carla, and Kassandra) I slept with in The Forsaken Years except for a one-night stand in Chicago, and with a black-haired Latina prostitute who called herself "Rose." I met "Rose" one night in Cicero, Illinois, when I accompanied a buddy to a bar that he frequented on occasion, more out of curiosity than a determination to pay for sex. We sat at the bar for about a half hour nursing a beer and staving off advances and temptation until he slipped away into a private room with a bed. A few minutes later, I gave in to Rose's charms and agreed to a "suck and a fuck" in the back room while sitting on a chair. Three, maybe five, minutes later I was back at the bar waiting for my pal. We soon departed, myself $40 poorer, a chunk torn from my conscience and a hole in my heart.

I almost slept with a married woman one night, the wife of a truck driver that worked where a buddy worked in my hometown. Things got playful one night after work at a bowling alley, then more intimate later at his house. She offered up her place because she thought her husband was out on the road. In my mind I was just giving her a ride home but I couldn't be sure until we turned onto her street and she saw her husband's car in the driveway; he got home early from his run. Thus, I was spared an encounter that I would have terribly regretted and can therefore recall with a shred of dignity how her large breasts and nipples felt to my hands between threads of high-count cotton and a non-padded silk bra.

I returned to Chicago because there was construction work there. Acting was now on a back burner with a blown fuse. Within a couple of months, my dad had a stroke and was hospitalized, in December 1989. I rushed home from Chicago on a Greyhound on December 21.

On the bus I wrote a poem:

Southern sun shines warm through the winter
  window
On the face of a chosen son.
An old man snores from across the aisle
And snares the mind of the chosen son
Snared in memories of a man
Who snored in peace in his favorite chair
In front of the TV
In his home.
An old woman reads in the seat before him,
Through black-framed glasses like yours,
A Catholic newspaper
Folded subway-style, Greyhound-style,
The style a man once showed his city-bound chosen
  son.
For mom's sake I hope that's not your soul passing,
All these snares and images.

You're lying in a hospital bed right now, aren't you?
You're probably going to be all right, aren't you?
Dad.
It's the shortest day of the year today,
Don't let it be the darkest, too.
I'm afraid.
I love you dad.
I want to say it a million more times.
Dad.
I'm your chosen son, your privileged son, your
   grateful son.
Your days may be winter days now,
Less intense are the rays,
But that golden sun outside, still bright, still warm,
   still shines.

Dad's stroke turned out to be mild, with only slight visible effects on the left side of his face. I included the poem because, as I was flipping through some writing I did at that time, I was struck by my referring to myself as a "chosen son," clearly a nod to my Catholic upbringing and adoption. I felt blessed to have been adopted by my mom and dad, I adored them, as is evidenced by Mother's Day and Father's Day poems I wrote earlier that same year – which makes me think that I should include, as an appendix, more of the poetry I wrote in the 80's and 90's. We'll see. It's also clear from those poems exactly how restless and homeless I felt.

It must have been at this time, while home visiting dad, when I read in the help wanted classifieds of the Des Moines Register that a representative of a commercial fishing operation based in Seattle, Washington, was going to be taking applications and interviewing prospects in a conference room at the downtown Holiday Inn during the coming weekend. I suppose to my restless heart that was akin to offering a sushi chef a sharper knife. I filled out the application and talked to the man but wasn't offered a job on the spot. What the hell!

So I went about my life, meaning I loaded up the backpack and took the Greyhound back to Chicago where my cousin let me crash on the floor of a bedroom in a house he was rehabbing on the north side, near Belmont and Damen Avenues. I remember that corner because there was a diner there on the southeast corner that served up a breakfast special for about $1.50. There was a bar a block away called The Augenblick that had traditional Irish music every Tuesday night.

Anyway, after about six Sundays of reading my poems at The Green Mill Lounge Poetry Slam, I got a call from the commercial fishing company asking me if I'd like to work for them… in Alaska.

The deal was, I'd have to sign a three-month contract, in exchange for which they'd fly me from Chicago to Anchorage where I'd catch a 14-seat prop plane to Dutch Harbor, about halfway out along the Aleutian Islands in the Bering Sea. I'd live rent-free on a commercial fishing vessel and all my meals would be provided. When the three months expired, or, more accurately, whenever the current expedition I was working on ended after three months had expired, they would pay for my flight home or wherever I wanted to go. The hiring guy on the phone made sure to mention that many fishermen opt to take a free flight to Hawaii for a long vacation, then get flown back to Dutch Harbor for another contract.

I went.

I'm trying to think of one word to describe my Alaskan Bering Sea fishing adventure. Despair comes to mind, but I wasn't a slave and I knew there was an out, short of death. There is an element of hopelessness that comes with despair, and truly almost every single time I woke up for a haul or shift in the two plus months that I "fished" it seemed hopeless that I'd find any joy, let alone peace. And anyway, when a person can despair of not finding a parking place within a hundred yards of the door at Costco, or of thirty-degree temperatures lingering into May in the Midwest, the word "despair" lacks that punch-to-the-throat kind of meaning I'm looking for.

Drudgery is certainly apt but doesn't quite reach the level of exactitude I'm striving for. I had a summer job in college where I worked for a neighbor on the farm he owned outside of town. We spent a couple days walking a few hundred acres of soybeans, cutting down weeds with a scythe. If I did that for two months without a break it would be drudgery, but I'd be outside, walking steadily on tilled black dirt, feeding off the sun and wind and birdsong and cloud formations, transitioning from trousers wet with dew to wet with sweat. I'd eat my lunch in the shade under a tree, or back in the farmhouse when the just-picked sweet corn is pulled from the pot ready to melt butter. There'd be a cold 16-ounce can of beer or two waiting for me at the end of the day on the wraparound porch as the sun gets low in the western sky. Sign me up for that gig and I might not even need the flight to Hawaii in three months.

The word that seems most applicable to working in a floating seafood processing factory disguised as a commercial fishing boat, manned by pricks in the frigid turbulent northern Pacific Ocean that would just as soon bury you as give up its treasure, is misery.

I'm merely trying to paint a picture because words are so subjective. One person's misery may simply be another person's challenge. And I understand that there is a difference between a misery like being born in South Sudan or losing a child when compared to a self-induced misery like I'm describing. But if writers had to compose under the weight of judgment or comparison, Amazon might have never had a book to sell in 1995, and then where would we be?

Thinking about it for just a minute, this doesn't seem like an issue for a painter or composer or sculptor. They can pour their thoughts and feelings out onto the canvas or score or stone and we bring our own experience to the relationship knowing that whatever we feel is valid, regardless of what the creator intended. So often, words get in the way or just ruin everything. Thus, a writer must, to a degree, overcome that feeling one has in a group therapy session that their truth isn't your truth and their story isn't worthy; my trauma isn't like your trauma, my abuse wasn't anything like your abuse.

All this to avoid writing about "fishing" in Alaska, as if just putting it down on paper will somehow make it real again.

It has taken me three days to get on with this. Seriously, I haven't touched this manuscript for three days because I just don't want to get into the seaweeds of the Alaska commercial fishing experience. Maybe I can devote…oh, bad word choice when writing about this.

Try again. Maybe I can flush through the scupper of my soul a few paragraphs for each of the boats I worked on and call it good. If nothing else, I may deter someone from thinking it's a good idea.

The first boat was a long liner, manned by a crew of about twelve to fifteen guys with names like Buck, Reno, Rambo, Slayer, Hollywood, Chico and Stretch. I probably knew the real names of some of the guys. Shawn and Scott are the only ones I remember. I'll talk about Scott at length in a minute. I almost killed Shawn and myself one night and that's why I remember his name.

Shawn and I were tasked with setting the flags and bags for the start of a set. A "set" is a long line of baited hooks…you see, there's no way to talk about this without getting into the details about "flags and bags," and just how long is that set line which is roughly fifty 600-foot sections of rope knotted together end-to-end, laced by 10,000 ganglions 40 inches apart with hooks on the end baited with thawed squid.

It makes my feet hurt to think about the way the baiting station was set up. A person had to stand on the edge of a length of 90-degree angle iron that dug into the soles of the feet. But that wasn't bad after a couple hours because the feet become numb from standing in oftentimes ankle-deep freezing sea water. To give an insight into the mind of the deck boss and captain, they held back about 20 brand new coco mats we could have been standing on to cushion our feet until the trip was about two days from completion.

It was the middle of the night. I was awakened by the deck boss, Buck, which after three or four fist pounds on the door, went something like this, "Get the fuck out of the rack! Bags and flags in ten minutes!" So, three weeks into the trip, half asleep, Shawn and I scramble up topside where the flags and bags are positioned, to wait for the captain's signal to throw the things overboard and initiate the set. I thought I saw the signal, Shawn didn't. I threw the flag (basically a buoy with a tall flag like a golf pin attached) early without realizing Shawn and I were standing on the line that was seconds from being drawn out to sea through the setting chute by the rapidly moving boat. He threw the bags and we jumped off just in time to avoid being flung out, tangled up in line, hooks and squid and plunged about 500 fathoms deep. No one would have known until we came up missing a couple hours later when it was time to "haul gear" (pull up a previously set line). Shawn cussed me up and down. We both were pretty shook up, understandably. In the end, he was pretty cool about it and he was one of two dudes I actually had conversations with during my time on the boat.

I couldn't have had less respect for the captain, or pilot, or whatever he was called. I only saw him up close a couple of times in the galley. Rumor had it he kept a gun in the wheelhouse. He also kept the seasickness patches up there where, apparently, he only gave them out to new guys, "greenies," after they'd been throwing up for about 36 hours. Now, if you were a captain, wouldn't you say to your deck boss, "Hey, keep an eye on the greenies once we leave Dutch Harbor. If any of them start looking nauseous, come get a patch from me. Let them know to ask you for one in case you miss the signs." A commonsense directive, it seems to me. Instead, I spent the entire trip to Attu, out at the very tip of the Aleutian Islands where we loaded bait, either puking or curled up in the fetal position on my bunk. They finally gave me a patch after the bait was loaded and we were headed out to sea. The "captain" also didn't seem to mind throwing any and all garbage off the boat into the ocean; plastic, useless rope, broken hooks, cardboard boxes, etc. I was appalled. Can you imagine? The man makes his living off what he can reap from the ocean, and he lets that go on? It would be like a rancher setting traps in the pasture where the cattle graze, or a farmer changing the oil and flushing the fluids from all his machines in his fields, every day.

We were fishing for the lucrative sablefish, or black cod, which just so happens to be a staple of orcas. Our trip was haunted by a pod of orcas that swam and cavorted on the surface about a quarter mile from the boat. Once they heard the hydraulics kick in, which signified the beginning of a haul, they disappeared. When the line came up, every time, the sablefish were picked clean off the hooks with only the odd head to show for what might have been. I should have been pissed since I was working for a percentage of the value of the catch, but I was secretly happy that the ocean was fighting back, and the whales were dining on our catch. The captain ended up abandoning the sablefish and instead filled the boat with the much cheaper gray cod, which orca is too picky to eat. We off-loaded the frozen slabs of fish onto a Japanese freighter to be used as cat food in Asia.

I have here in my notes that the boat was a former transport ship for dead servicemen in the Pacific Theater during WWII before it was fitted out as a fish factory. My dad served in a medical unit in the Pacific and quite possibly had a hand in easing the suffering of men that would eventually find their way home on that ship.

As is usually true, humor can often be found amidst pain and suffering. It is perfectly fitting that the only humor found on that ship involved someone else's pain. Again, from the notes, Rambo fell in the galley one time when the ship listed suddenly and violently, sending him on his ass beneath his tray and two steaks. Once, on a particularly nasty day with the boat getting tossed around, one of the experienced crew members sent a greenie out on the deck with a Hefty bag and a zip tie and told him to get a fog sample and take it to the captain. Another time, again on a nasty day, a greenie was told to go out on the deck and watch for the mail buoy. And this last one from my notes, a greenie was told to go out and stand on the bow with a flag in hand so the captain could conduct a wind test.

This isn't in my notes, but I remember it clearly. There was a couple on the boat, not married. She was about five months pregnant, but you'd hardly know it if you didn't know it. She was a baiter like I was. I don't recall what her guy did on the boat. I remember she was a baiter because I used to help her when I could; I'd often carry her tub, heavy with line she'd just baited, over to where they were stationed near the setting chute. One day I awakened from a few hours of sleep to learn that she'd had a miscarriage on the boat and was gone, along with her partner. I think she was airlifted off the boat by the Coast Guard, but I'm not 100% sure of that. I'd like to think I'd have heard a helicopter hovering above the boat.

No, I wouldn't have. I slept with earplugs stuffed so far into my head I could hear a fart twenty minutes before it passed my sphincter. The only time I didn't wear earplugs was when I ate or showered. The assault on the soul was equally matched by the assault on the ears; heavy metal music on blown speakers playing nonstop in the work area, hydraulics, engines, people shouting, etc. My mom grew up in the Depression Era and hoarded canned goods to the point where one had to open the pantry door in our kitchen very slowly and be ready to grab anything that might come falling. I hoarded earplugs on the boat; in my notes it says that I left after about a one-month tour on that long liner with over 50 unused pairs in my duffle bag.

⁂

 I also left that boat with a really good friend that I made on the very first day when I was deposited in my cabin by Buck, the deck boss, who had picked me and a couple others up at the Dutch Harbor airport. It turned out he had picked up a couple other greenies at the airport earlier in the day. One of them was Scott McBurney.

 Scott was from Denver, Colorado. He had answered a help wanted ad like mine because he thought he could make a lot more money than he had currently been earning as a Gray Line tour bus driver, and he liked adventure. We were the same age. When we met in our shared cabin, I was holding my copy of Walt Whitman's "Leaves of Grass" and he had just come from the galley toting a copy of the collected works of William Butler Yeats. When we noticed this in the same instant, we knew we'd be friends for life. I mean, what were the chances that probably the only two sorry ass sons of bitches that had volumes of poetry in the entire vastness of the Bering Sea fishing industry were bunkmates in the same cabin?

Scott received his master's degree in music performance from Texas Christian University and competed in the Van Cliburn International Piano Competition there. He was a freaking concert pianist or could have been!

"What the hell was he doing on this boat?" you might be asking. I never had to ask. I knew. He and I were brothers of the spirit and soul.

Here's two guys with artistic temperaments working on a boat with mostly thugs, racists, and homophobes. As I mentioned, I was a baiter. Scott worked on the freezer crew with a lying, lazy, ass-clown I only knew as Reno, alternating between bringing up frozen cases of bait to be thawed or replacing the void with similar sized freezer bags of frozen fish. It's amazing how little our paths crossed on that boat. But the routines of our respective jobs, by nature, almost required working opposite times.

We made the most of the time we had with great conversations. Neither of us could fathom how we were going to endure three months on that boat. Then something amazing happened. We had pillaged the Bering Sea for about a month, until the hold was fully stuffed with frozen slabs of cod, turbot and redfish. Back at Dutch Harbor during the offload, we learned that the company had another boat, a trawler, preparing to go out to sea. We put in for a transfer and got it. We packed our bags, gathered our outerwear and wellies and, practically giddy, toted them over to the trawler. We got a cabin assignment together, then went and bought four oil-can-sized Foster's Lagers and walked up a hill and drank them while overlooking the harbor and the ominous flotilla of maritime menace docked there. It would have been beautiful if we didn't know what went on in those motherfucking boats. I remember we talked about going to a Seattle Mariners game when we finished our "tour."

By the way, I'm listening to Johannes Brahms music exclusively while I remember Scott. Brahms was his favorite composer and it was his music he played at the Cliburn Competition.

The trawler was more of a grind. I obtained a seasickness patch straight away. Scott and I worked side-by-side selecting fish that came along the conveyor, beheading and gutting them before tossing them across a stainless-steel partition to three Japanese guys who put them into pans according to size and weight, then to be flash frozen and sent to the hold. We were fishing for one species only, so anything that the trawler pulled up in that enormous net that wasn't what we wanted, went dead along the conveyor out a chute back into the ocean. Sixteen-hour shifts with a half-hour meal break after eight hours. Then eight hours to eat the other two meals before and after whatever sleep one could snag. Fatigue led to irritability which often led to perceived slights and short fuses, which led one day to a shoving match that Scott, and hence I, got into with the guys to Scott's right (I was on his left), each of us with our gutting knives in our hands. I no longer recall what started it or how it ended, but I do remember thinking, "That could have been really ugly!"

There actually were moments when a guy could steal away topside and catch a sunset or sunrise, or simply stare off beyond the horizon, gaze at the stars. Life on the trawler was not nearly as miserable as it was on the long liner. But as we neared the end of the tour, as the hold neared its capacity, Scott and I decided we'd had enough of the fishing experience. We offloaded to another Japanese freighter, collected our meager paychecks, and paid for our own flights back to Scott's hometown of Denver because we didn't fulfill our three-month commitment. Financially, I broke even; the orcas, it turned out, were as good at picking pockets as they were at picking black cod off fishing line.

To this day, I've never been so glad to get away from a place. You'd think I'd have taken my green Helly Hansen rain jacket and bib overalls and burned them along with my rubber wellies in the first dumpster I encountered in Denver, but I kept them. I still have them, down in the garage, and I bet if I soaked the inside of the jacket and scratched hard enough, I could smell the fish and the sea and the pain. How I've kept them all these years is pretty goddamn amazing when I think of it. I can still read where I wrote "Irish" with a black Sharpie along the upper edge of my wellies one of the first days I'd begun this wild adventure because so many guys had nicknames and if I could have one, I'd want it to represent my adopted heritage and spiritual motherland. It didn't work, I was always Greenie.

***

I spent a few days in Denver with Scott, staying at his dad's house. We hit some great bookstores, ate amazing food at Mexican restaurants and at his sister's apartment, drove up into the mountains, and took in Boulder. Rumor has it we drank some beer; my memory is foggy on that score. When I left the Mile High City, we didn't need to say, "Let's keep in touch." We were friends for life, my Camerado.

12
"You're One of Us"

I stopped at home to see mom and dad before moving on back to Chicago. The stroke and the scare had taken their toll on both. They seemed to have aged more than ever in the few months since I'd seen them. Before I left for Chicago, I wrote this poem titled, *"To the Little Lad."*

Could the little lad have looked at me today like I saw him?
Oh, how can he see places that his life has never been?
Only age allows an older man to fondly look behind at a little lad and lovely lady walking hand in hand.
And what if I'd have seen that man when I's a little lad.
Oh, how could I have known that that ol' man was really sad?
Only age allows an older man to fully understand the pain that comes from looking back upon a little lad.
But a little lad did look at me today, and I saw him.
With a longing in his eyes, I felt him say, "Where have you been?"
Only age allows a little lad to know what the old man knows, and why the eyes of the old man cry at the voice he hears within, when to the little lad I hear him say again, "Where did you go?"

In Chicago that spring and summer, I got a job working as a union laborer on the renovation of the historic Rookery Building downtown. It was hard work and I was paid well. Along about mid-summer, with a nicely growing bank account, I decided it was time; I called home and told mom and dad to get passports. Ireland was calling, louder than ever, and I was taking them with me. We'd leave in September.

It was like I was studying for the LSAT the way I read up on Ireland in the months and years leading up to this trip; Joyce and Wilde, Yeats and Kavanagh, "Twenty Years A-Growing," Leon Uris' "Trinity," a history of Ireland. Imagine my amazement when, at the rental car counter at Shannon Airport, we were offered a free upgrade if we passed the Limerick Scribe Admissions Test by reeling off six poems. I looked left. I looked right. I shook off my jetlag and said to my mom and dad, "I got this."

To hear a Hibernian voice,
I thought I would read me some Joyce.
His prose is foreboding!
My head is exploding!
What's up with his fecking word choice? *
*I came up with this when recalling once trying to read "Finnegan's Wake."

When ordering fresh pints of Guinness,
There's only one order of business:
Make sure above all,
To not miss last call,

And order 'fore everyone's finished. *

*Composed while recalling a night of debauchery when, eight pints and a shot of Bushmills into a long night at a pub in Chicago listening to traditional music, I staggered legless and bleary-eyed back to my cousin's house certain the aroma from a nearby chimney was actually smoke from a thatched roof cottage's turf fire.

On the Ha'penny Bridge 'cross the Liffey,
I suddenly needed the biffy.
Should I just whip it out,
And pass all that stout,
Or get to the pub in a jiffy? *

*Composed when I learned the car rental agent was a former rugby player from Dublin.

A fella named Paddy McTurloch
Owned him a fine fish and chip shop.
In west Erin fair
It's the only one there
With three Michelin stars and a windsock. *

*Composed while observing a food service van speeding down the tarmac.

There once was a Clare gal from Ennis,
In love with the priest/herder Seamus.
She wore woolen knickers,
And ignored all the snickers,
Whenever the priest rang the Ang'lus. *

*Composed after glimpsing the front page of the Irish Sun newspaper in the bin.

Ted brought to the County Clare ceili,
His spoons and a teak ukulele.
The fiddler's laughter
Rattled the rafters
And shattered three bottles of whiskey. *

*Composed when I recalled a conversation two gents were having in the loo before clearing customs.

The lad behind the counter was gobsmacked. Then, in what I'd come to learn is typical of Irishmen, he challenged me to up my game. He said, "If you can come up with a two-stanza limerick in 60 seconds, I'll comp your rental and make it a Mercedes-Benz 560 SL."

I burned ten seconds thinking, then said, "Get the keys…"

A burly Nebraska Cornhusker
Fell hard for a Grafton Street busker.
He missed the big game
Against Notre Dame
While he mustered the courage to ask her.

'Twas a paean of marriage proposals
'Till he asked, "Do you understand football?"
The Yank struck a nerve,
What a lesson he learned,
When she struck her left boot to his jewels. *

*(Mic drop) Mom, dad and I left the rental car counter with honors and a personal escort to the M18.

Actually, we picked up our modest four-door Opel and within an hour we were pulling into the car park at Bunratty Castle and Folk Park, the first stop on a two-week tour of Eireann.

I should mention an event that foreshadowed my dad's emotional arc in the fortnight that ensued when, as he reached up to stow his carry-on bag in the overhead bin, his pants fell around his ankles. Because of his "Irish ass", there wasn't much flesh behind his hips (he hadn't yet taken to wearing suspenders). When his arms went high, his trousers went low.

We hit all the touristy spots on our way south along the west coast, dad in the front seat, mom in the back with her journal. It was delightful, September, the summer rush of tourists all but gone and the island mostly to us. We circled south and saw Cork and Kinsale, up the east coast through Waterford and Wicklow, skirted around Dublin, then headed northwest to County Sligo before journeying south again through Mayo and Galway and back to Clare and Shannon Airport.

County Mayo was always in our sights, which is why we left it near the end of the tour. My dad's father was born in a little village called Murrisk on the southern shore of Clew Bay, almost at the base of Croagh Patrick. Dad had a first cousin whose son ran a pub in Westport. He had another first cousin that still lived in the house where his father, my grandfather, was born and had lived before he went away to serve with an Irish regiment in WWI, before he emigrated to the U.S. We arrived in Westport and immediately went to the pub for supper and pints, not in that order, met the cousins, and planned to go to the original homestead the following afternoon.

First stop was the Murrisk Abbey and cemetery where we had no problem finding old grave markers with the family name etched and time worn in granite. We then went across the road, parked at the end of the driveway, and knocked on the door of my grandfather's homestead. A younger cousin opened the door and invited us into the kitchen where my dad's first cousin, Michael, sat beside a stove in a tattered and worn out burgundy Irish sweater. That stove might have been the only heat source in the house. We all sat around the kitchen table where the younger cousin produced glasses and a bottle of Irish whiskey. No ice. Could it be more perfect?

Michael Geraghty was old. The scattered dandruff on his shoulders reminded me of the flakes of dried sea salt one finds on the round crust of a loaf of dark rye. His voice was quiet and lacked the air it needed to carry it to my dad's ears in a steady flow. Paired with his thick accent, my dad really struggled to understand what Michael was saying. When I retold the story of how, when he was a little lad, Michael remembered my grandfather coming home from WWI on horseback, my dad, himself a veteran, wept. What a moment! It was the highlight of the entire trip, and I felt so happy and proud that I had made it happen for both my mom and my dad.

Michael was also tired. Our visit ended too soon. His son walked with us out to the end of the driveway. We hugged and shook hands and expressed our gratitude for their warmth and hospitality. When my dad turned to look upon the homestead one last time, at the threshold his father had crossed on a day so long ago when he left home for America, as his cousin walked slowly away, he was overcome with emotion. As dad cried, his shoulders shook, his chest and belly heaved, and his pants fell down round his ankles.

In the few days that remained, we marveled at the beauty of Connemara, walked the streets of Galway City and the strand at Salthill, and had our breath stolen by the windy and wildly stunning west coast of Clare.

It was a very special time, sharing every moment of every day together, the trip of a lifetime. Two weeks of Cead Mile Failte and Irish breakfasts, pubs, photo ops, narrow roads and motorways, and occasional hot water bottles in beds. We'd do it all again in two years with their best friend and neighbor, Ray, the beer distributor I worked for back in the day. But for now, I walked with them as far as customs at Shannon, cried my eyes out as I hugged them both farewell and walked away with my backpack over my shoulder to begin my own journey around Ireland and points east across the Irish Sea.

My dad was 100% Irish, in that his dad and grandparents were all born in Ireland. My mom was about 25% Irish, but when she married, it was as if her DNA was poured into a centrifuge and the German and English elements spun away, leaving only a few strains with names like sauerbraten, speck und eier, stollen and apfelkuchen. St. Patrick's Day in my house growing up was as big a deal as Thanksgiving; mom cooking and baking all day, Irish music on the turntable in the living room, the wearing of the green. Going to Ireland was like a pilgrimage for them, and Murrisk was their Mecca.

As I've said, Ireland was my adopted motherland and my spiritual home. I guess that's the beauty of being adopted as an infant; at some point one gets to choose what they want to be until they learn differently. I chose to be 100% Irish, although realizing I didn't have an "Irish ass" made me consider I might have some Viking blood in me. But all things considered, I was proud to call the land of poets, Potato Famine and subjugation survivors, writers, and Guinness home.

If it wouldn't be such an utter and complete travesty and theft of a most beautiful anthem, I might take the Nina Simone song, "Young, Gifted and Black," and transcribe it into something like, "Young, Irish and Back." And now I'm thinking so much of my story could be titled, "Young, Privileged and White." I've tried to keep politics and cultural zeitgeist out of the telling here, but at the moment it seems impossible. This is not an apology, nor am I ashamed of my race, but the fact is that I couldn't have done most of what I did in "The Forsaken Years" had I been black. I'll leave it at that and get back to the road.

In my memory, I walked from Shannon Airport to the town of Gort, in County Galway; a quick query into Google Maps shows that it is 31 miles. I didn't do that in one day after leaving my mom and dad…did I? I do know that I booked a room in Gort because my feet were in tatters from walking. The next day I caught a bus to Galway City, changed buses and continued north to Westport and checked into the hostel on the outskirts of town.

I whiled away the days in Westport writing poetry, reading, and taking long walks around the countryside. In the evenings I sought out traditional music in the local pubs and, failing that, or in addition to that, continued what was becoming the delicious burden I felt I owed to myself as a self-proclaimed Irishman, which was to determine which brewery's stout I preferred most, Guinness, Murphy's or Beamish.

I pretty much had the hostel to myself, Westport being off the beaten path and it getting on toward the end of September. It was during this time that a woman named Marilyn from Anchorage, Alaska, arrived at the hostel. She was backpacking all over Ireland and we struck up an easy friendship. The next day she continued up the west coast to Donegal but said she'd be back in Westport in a few days. When she returned, I was still around doing my thing as before, so she joined me for an evening on the "Which Stout Is Better and At Which Pub" tour. That night we took a tour of each other's bodies in the hostel room I had all to myself. The next morning, after exchanging addresses, she traveled on. I decided it was time to do the same. We said our farewells and I never saw her again. We corresponded off and on for several years, up until about four years ago. And in what is either the strangest of coincidences or proof that mental energies travel hundreds of miles to their specific targets, I was asked a few days ago to become Facebook friends with Marilyn, who now resides in Colorado. (I'm adding this last bit during a final edit, about two weeks after "finishing" the manuscript.)

Before Marilyn left, she insisted I do myself a favor and travel to a tiny village on the coast of Clare called Doolin. She told me it was the best place in Ireland to hear traditional music and that there are amazing musicians playing in one of the three pubs every night and that there were two hostels to choose from. I tucked that information away for the time being and plotted my overland travels to Greece with my ever-present companion, Wanderlust.

Why Greece, you ask? Simple. A fantastic actor and friend of mine from Chicago was a Greek-American guy named Michael Raysses. I loved the stories of his immigrant family in Indiana, his humor, and the fact that he earned a law degree and set it aside to be an actor. He always called me Kid. He gave me a book to read by Henry Miller about a man's travels around Greece titled "The Colossus of Maroussi." When I read it, I remember thinking how great it would be to see that country. The time was nigh upon me.

I knew there was a train out of Westport that could take me to Dublin. From there, I took a train to Rosslare where I booked deck passage on an overnight ferry to Le Havre, France. The next day, I hitchhiked to Paris and spent a couple nights in a hostel while I paid my respects to the Left Bank, cafes, the Mona Lisa, and La Tour Eiffel. From there, I took the train third/economy/cattle car class across Europe for Athens, with a couple connections to make along the way, one for several hours in Belgrade. I remember sleeping there in the middle of the night outside under a station awning, sitting on my backpack with my back to a brick wall.

That rail journey was something like two days of grand soliturowded exhilaraustion and I swear I'd do it again tomorrow if the opportunity arose. There's nothing like a train, even if smoking was allowed in those days! Eastern Europeans smoked like crazy and the rail cars and compartments at times were choked with burning tobacco. So what! When it got too bad, I would exit the compartment and I'd fold down a round tiny aisle seat from its recess in the wall, crack a window, and watch the pastoral movie unfold outside.

I have no memory of the train station in Athens. I walked to a hostel where I got my own tiny room with not much more than space for a single bed and a desk. But it had a door that I could lock and a full bath down the hall. I was happy to be free of the big backpack and eager to eat and explore my way around antiquity.

It was early October 1990. I was 29 years old. It had been eighteen years and a few months since I learned of my adoption, when I was unmoored and set adrift by the unshakable idea that I wasn't the person I thought I was. I felt broken. And for all the joy and pain and miles, I was just trying to fix myself.

Motion, once like medicine, was producing some familiar side effects. The more I travelled, the more restless and homeless I felt. And while movement meant that I was going somewhere, doing something, I was feeling less like Meriwether Lewis and more like Sacagawea.

In Athens I was assuaged by things like seeing the sun rise and set from the Acropolis, sharing almost every meal in outdoor cafes with feral cats, buying leather sandals from the man who made them, having my hair cut and stubble shaved by a barber who didn't speak a word of English and tipping him lavishly. I shared beers with a Russian woman named Katrina in a taverna for several hours one evening and pleaded with her to run away with me to no avail because her father had made it possible for her to leave Russia and she couldn't bring herself to upset him. I started to leave but returned to steal a long and tender kiss goodbye and left with an aching heart.

In the depths of my being, I understood that relationships were the key to my resurrection from the loneliness and despair that gripped me at times. I was feeling things so deeply and intensely that oftentimes, in the throes of great natural or human beauty, I grieved over experiencing them alone.

I was a mess, really. When I was "with" myself, I was joyous, in terrific company. When I was "by" myself, I was alone.

In a state of loneliness, in the wake of those intense hours with Katrina, I wanted to get out of Athens. My cousin and my theater professor friend Doc had both been to Mykonos, so the next day I departed on a ferry for the island. I arrived at night, too late to find a place to stay or roll out a sleeping bag in the pitch-black darkness where there weren't sheep or dogs wandering about. I got kicked out of a nightclub for eating a baguette from my backpack, so I bought a few beers from a shop that was closing and sat at a table of theirs on the promenade, or whatever they called it. I stayed up all night sipping from green bottles and writing a letter to Katie while being stalked by men intrigued by my solitude. It had absolutely nothing to do with being stalked, but the next morning I boarded a ferry back to Athens and booked a train there to take me across the Peloponnese to Patras where I boarded another ferry to take me across the Adriatic Sea to Brindisi, Italy. Movement.

I blew west across Italy on the train, switched in Rome, and headed north for Munich for a couple of days of eating, drinking beer and walking around town. I stopped in Amsterdam for about six hours and I couldn't get a good vibe; the dudes in the packed and disheveled hostel seemed to resent my presence. I wasn't interested in experiencing hash bars or legal sex workers. There were things that interested me about Amsterdam, but at that point, I didn't want to work that hard. I was ready to get my wandering self to a place where I could settle for a couple of weeks and catch my breath. I walked back to the station and left on the next train to France. I was one more ferry ride away from Ireland. From there, a train ride west to Galway City and a bus from there to County Clare, Lisdoonvarna to be exact. From Lisdoon, I walked the few miles west to the coastal town, a village really, of Doolin. Doolin (the place Marilyn had told me about in Westport) in those days was nothing much more than three pubs, a shop with a post office, a pier, a gift shop, a cafe, two hostels and a Catholic church. I checked into the Doolin Hostel, clueless as to what an impact this tiny village would have on the course of my life for the next five years.

Now, as I look at Google Maps and YouTube videos of Doolin, I see that the Doolin Hostel is now an Inn getting over $150 per night. I don't recognize the village, what with all the new construction of hotels, pubs, and houses. I wonder what has changed more, it or me? From where I sit today and thinking back, I love them both, the way they were and the way they are.

Every portal to my soul was open in those days. In Ireland, in Doolin, by the sea, on the craggy shore, on the hillside green, looking west, soaked by the surf, bathed in light, lashed by wind and rain, warmed beside turf fires, amidst haunting strains of a people's musical yearning played for free, a day in the life of a chosen son.

I have an Irish passport and dual citizenship by virtue of my dad's dad being born in Ireland. But I truly became an Irish citizen in October 1990 in Doolin, baptized in the Atlantic Ocean, by my own hands, chieftain to a clan of one and allied to anyone who let me be.

Stand at sea level as the tide swells toward you as if to swallow you whole, a step or two closer than you dare stand having studied the waves break for an hour. What is an hour to this madness of timelessness before you? The surf pounds and crashes before you and explosions of ocean erupt around you from unseen tunnels out of fissures and holes in stone, portals from a time that Celts feared to fathom, and you too may be baptized.

It was with this sense of awe and wonder and rebirth that I met Ted McCormac at the Doolin Hostel when he came to stay with his daughter and little grandchildren over the October Bank Holiday weekend. If I was newly baptized and Irish, then Ted was my godfather, or at the very least, my confirmation sponsor.

Odd thought: Christianity appropriated or adapted many of its stories and rituals from the pagans and "non-believers" that it converted. So, it is amusing to me, a non-religious person, that I'm using Christian ideas and rituals as metaphors where it suits me for what I experienced.

But back to Ted. Everything that I felt about my Irishness, my identity, was validated and supported by Ted, as Dublin as any man could be. Of course, he knew I was an American; neither of us was denying that. But it was through Ted that I heard the words I'll never forget. We were sitting around a cluster of tables with a bunch of locals at a favorite Dublin pub of his called Sean O'Casey's, taking turns singing songs, when one of the old Dublin ladies, a Mrs. May in my notes, said to me, "You're one of us." Those four words cut through almost twenty years of longing and planted themselves in a heart now open and at peace. My eyes welled up with tears, and maybe a touch of the elixir from St. James's Gate, when Ted said, "It's true, Tom."

Ted let me live with him for months after my second trip to Ireland with my mom and dad two years later. He never once asked for an Irish pound or pence. As a matter of fact, he greeted us at Dublin Airport when we arrived for that holiday and was our personal escort around the town for two days! Twenty-four years my elder, he was more a friend than a father figure. We are friends to this day, we talk on the phone, and my life is so much richer for the time and love and selfless generosity he bestowed upon me.

Ted was proud to be Irish and it rubbed off on me. I remember the day he took me to a long-deserted famine village (think ghost town) tucked away in the barren limestone Burren north of Doolin. It was just a tight-knit cluster of former stone huts, with gravity, weather and vegetation the only inhabitants. Standing amidst those roofless ruins, I felt a oneness with the long-gone clan impossible to describe.

I was a boy again, experiencing things for the first time or in a new way. I had seen the night sky from a boat in the middle of the ocean and it was amazing; I expected that. But seeing the night sky, moonless, with my feet on the earth, on the west coast of Ireland with an ocean pounding the shore before me, the unamplified music of a people still ringing in my ears, an absence of electric light behind me, it was primal, like stepping through a portal to another time.

And speaking of portals: sitting six feet away from a music circle, watching and hearing musicians play from their souls the songs of their lives with a brilliance and current that connects the ages, produced in me a feeling that came to me like love. That connection hit its peak in McGann's Pub in Doolin, listening to Ted and friends play. While a man named Peadar Reilly gave us "Inisheer" on his tin whistle, I sat there at my tiny pub table, solitary amidst the crowd, and let tears flow freely and unswept down into my beard.

13

Das Wasser

I turn to a favorite metaphor for a life, a river, to help me describe the mental and physical state I was in when Kassandra came into my life.

My banks were full of a sense of belonging, the flow as calm and balanced as I'd known since I was a boy. Imagine a river away from civilization, in early summer after the winter's thaw and the torrents of spring rains have abated, able to receive all that it generously encounters while containing all that it has been. Amidst the weeping of willows, graceful to the winding whims of the world, there are no constructs to destroy, no reapings to ruin. In that current moment, things once deemed foreign to the reach vie and breach and strive to bring meaning and sentiment to the stream to be held and carried there forever. Or until the next flood.

Kassandra entered my stream in early December 1992. As I mentioned, I had taken my mom and dad back to Ireland, along with their friend Ray McHenry, for two weeks in October. (In case you've been wondering all this time where Ray's wife has been, she died when I was five years old. I vividly remember asking my mom and dad at the dinner table on my sixth birthday where Mrs. McHenry was and when they told me she died, I cried. It's the first time I remember crying for someone that died, Mary Jane McHenry, my mom's best friend.)

I stayed in Ireland after mom, dad and Ray went home and was living with Ted in his apartment in Dublin. These were wonderful weeks living in a great city with an even greater friend.

One weekend, Ted and a slew of his friends and relations, mostly Dubliners, decided to caravan to Doolin for a holiday and they brought me along. We left Dublin on Thursday afternoon, packed into three cars like knights on a westward crusade to conquer in varying degrees of importance as many tunes, pints and, for some, pairs of knickers as an Irish bachelor could handle. We stopped at a relative of Ted's house outside Roscommon for a night of music and drinking, followed by a restless sleep on the floor of the sitting room, looking like casualties in a field hospital, and arrived in Doolin midday Friday. Some checked into the old hostel on the Aille River. I chose my old haunt at the Doolin Hostel. Some took naps, others did whatever, with the understanding we would all meet up in one of the pubs that night. I chose to take a bit of saunter over to the Doolin Pier, wander along the coast for a bit, then venture over to McGann's Pub where I knew there'd be a turf fire to sit beside while drinking a well-earned pint and writing a letter home.

I was deep into letter writing when a woman with a German accent asked if she could join me at my table by the fire to warm and dry herself after a long walk along the coast; it had been raining since I had arrived at the pub. That woman was Kassandra.

First impressions: she was a woman; she spoke English with a German accent…allow me to recall that summer of my youth when a girl named Meike from Hamburg, Germany, spent a month with the Daniels family next door, to remember how I spent one evening under the stars lying on a trampoline with her and couldn't get up the nerve to ask for a kiss, to rue how she was gone one day with no fanfare, never to be seen again? I don't believe it's much of a stretch to say Kassandra's voice hit upon a tender place in the recesses of my heart.

When she asked to share my table by the fire, I simply said, "Sitenzie downheit und maken zieselfunzie ut homenschlafen."

Well, it didn't go quite like that. I welcomed her to the small table and made room for her by moving my things over to my side. I don't recall what we talked about, only that the talk came easy. I remember after a while we went for a walk, spent the evening together in the pub and I spent the next two nights in her room at a bed and breakfast across the road where she had arranged a long-term rental during the off-season.

I didn't see much of the lads that weekend. Sunday afternoon I reunited with the caravan back to Dublin, enduring a fair share of good-natured teasing over my "conquest" of Casablanca, so called because Noel Quinn couldn't remember the name Kassandra. I had an uneasy feeling even then. I didn't, or couldn't, read the signs enough to fully understand that my river was forked.

One sign I failed to pick up on was how I wished I had hung out with the lads. Kassandra and I had nice walks, great conversations, sex, but I kept wondering what Ted and the guys were up to. And the vibe at the B and B was downright chilly; the owners kicked Kassandra out after I left on Sunday for sleeping in the room with a man out of marriage; totally their right to do that, what with children in the home and being Catholic and all.

The thing is, I liked Kassandra. And there was that whole notion I had of honor and decency when it came to that most intimate of encounters between two people. I don't regret ever feeling that way, but in Kassandra's case, having sex might have prevented me from casually walking away; I know it did. Kassandra was strong, independent and smart, but there was a woundedness about her that attracted me like a finger to a splinter; you sense there's something there but you can't really see it, there's a weight to the wood, the surface is a little rough, it's been cut yet still smells pretty sweet, but eventually, when you go to set it down, it snags you under the nail.

It took almost three years to separate myself from her. In the end, in 1995 and living in Berlin for the second winter, depressed and harboring thoughts of suicide, I knew I had to either leave her or lose myself forever. I wrote Kassandra a long letter goodbye and the next morning, after she left for her job caring for dependent adults, I showered, packed what I wanted, left the rest, and fled the apartment. My flight wasn't until the next day, so I stashed my duffle bag under a bench in a cemetery across from an all-night tavern where I spent the night reading and drinking coffee. I arrived in Chicago and was met by my friend, Dan deRegnier, who lived in Big Rapids, Michigan. He and his wife, Jan, kindly let me stay with them for a week while I licked my wounds and got up the strength to go home.

In between that ending and the beginning, there were good times and strange times.

Christmas arrived about three weeks after Kassandra and I met. She wanted me to come to Doolin and spend the holiday with her. I chose to stay in Dublin because Ted invited me to have Christmas dinner with his wife (they had been separated for years) and four daughters — four single, attractive, my age or younger, daughters. I might have fallen hard for Rachel if I wasn't... and that server at the pub Ted and I went to and sang at together on some Sunday afternoons, I might have fallen hard for her if I wasn't... and that waitress at the golf club in Athenry, County Galway, where I worked as an assistant chef for several months in '94 when Kassandra and I were separated, I might have fallen hard for her if I wasn't...

I suppose, thinking about it like this for the first time, I might have Kassandra to thank for keeping me distracted long enough for me to make it back where I belonged, with Katie.

Shortly after that first Christmas (neither of us were practicing Catholics or even religious at this point), Kassandra and I decided to take Bus Eireann north to a tiny village on the coast of County Donegal named Glencolumbkille. She knew about a cottage beyond the pale of the village where we were booked to stay for a month or so to see if we were meant to be together. I was having my doubts, mainly because she had to hammer home the fact of how sad and lonely and disappointed she was that I chose Ted over her for the recent holiday. The fact was, I didn't feel guilty or have any regrets. And I knew guilt from growing up in an Irish Catholic home where, if I failed my mom in any way, she'd say to me, "Oh, you wouldn't walk across the street for yesterday's newspaper." And I still don't know what that means. In those days, in Des Moines, we got two newspapers delivered to our front door every day, The Register in the morning and The Tribune in the afternoon, and one on Sunday! Maybe it was a Chicago newsstand reference?

Glencolumbkille in January 1993 was, I imagine, pretty much the way it was in 1953. The one shop in the village was lit by a small bulb that hung by a wire in the middle of the ceiling. We spent our days walking along the coast, and trying to keep the turf fire lit in the fireplace because it was the only source of heat. (We went to sleep beside that hearth and woke with frost on our blanket, and that's no joke!) Did I mention that the cottage was damp?

After several days, the moment of truth for our relationship arrived. We decided to each go our own way for the day to search our souls, a practice we'd repeat the following winter in Portugal and one that I would perform in my mind dozens of times after this fateful first foray into the murky looking glass of liebe and lust. Honestly, trying to read my soul after Kassandra roiled my waters was akin to admiring the embers of a turf fire through a pint of Guinness. Anyway, we agreed to meet back at the cottage before dark, about 4:00 that far north. I decided to wear my wellies (from Alaska) because I figured at some point I'd be walking in tall grass by the shore.

I left the village along the road that led to the ocean. I walked slowly. I meandered along the shore and up on the bluffs. Finally, with no clear vision on what my heart desired, I decided to sit my ass down on a stony promontory that overlooked a kind of valley below. To my right was the ocean, to my left was the way back to the cottage.

I don't remember how long I sat there. The view was spectacular, but the mental anguish I was enduring was eating me up. Finally, after going back and forth as to whether I should stay with her or say farewell, entertaining pros and cons like a character in my own Shakespearean tragedy (call it the Lobe Theatre), I decided to stay with Kassandra and give the relationship the chance I reckoned it deserved.

With the decision made, I looked around to determine the best way off the height down to the valley floor. I could go back the way I came, but what fun is that? It didn't look too steep from where I sat, so I decided I could shimmy my way down on my ass to a sheep trail I spotted maybe fifty feet below me. About half-way down, still scooting on my butt like a crab, I lost my footing, skidded, dug my fingers into the stone to no avail, tried to get a grip with my wellies (they were useless), and went airborne, freefalling the final ten feet or so where I landed on the sheep trail and stuck there like my clothes and the path were made of Velcro. The trail was no more than 2 ½ feet wide. How I stopped, I have no idea. I lay there for several minutes collecting myself, looking around, feeling if anything was broken. Had I not stopped on the narrow strip of grass, I'd have plummeted bouncing off granite until I landed crushed, bloody, and most likely dead.

After taking stock of my bones and muscles, I slowly stood and followed the sheep trail to the valley floor. From there, I walked through the soggy overgrown bogland for a long stretch parallel to the road and back to the cottage where I stripped down and soaked in a hot bath until Kassandra returned.

"Tis meself here now and I be wonderin, tinkin' I must have had on me Irish woolen jumper or that sheep trail would have never held me, sure." Truth is, I very well might have been wearing one of my authentic Irish woolen mill crafted sweaters, jumpers as they call them…wait a minute! Jumpers? Wouldn't it be ironic if I had died in that fall wearing a "jumper?" It begs the question, what do the Garda call a person standing on the rail of a bridge over the River Liffey? How do they call it in?

"Dispatch, we have a jumper on the O'Connell Street Bridge."

"Jaysus, Murphy, what are ye callin' me fer wit' dis? Try it on, fer feck's sake! If it fits just keep it, ya dopey shoit."

Tis a mystery.

Truth be told, and I'm back to being serious now, the question I was asking myself in the tub was this: did the fact that I fell and lived and didn't die at the bottom of the cliff where I likely wouldn't have been found for possibly days, have anything to do with my decision to stay in the relationship? Was survival an affirmation, or was falling a portent of future anguish? I must have determined it all to be an affirmation. When Kassandra returned, I downplayed the scrapes and bruises as being from a tumble and left it at that. We both professed our commitment to give our relationship a chance.

As I said, I gave it a chance for over two years. We went to Portugal for a month one winter, highlighted by drinking amazing and inexpensive wine, eating huge oranges right off the tree, enjoying warm weather, renting tandem bicycles in the Algarve, and getting into deep shit for saying she was "insatiable" one morning while on my way out the door to get some coffee. This was in response to her request of another romp, an English word she didn't know. When I defined insatiable, you'd have thought I called her a whore. We soon spent a day apart because we needed it (and something I've never needed in twenty-five years of marriage with Katie, but there it is).

We spent a few months in Des Moines our first summer together. I needed to make some money. I flew home solo, secured a house framing gig, and then sent for Kassandra a couple weeks later, picking her up at O'Hare International. She revealed to me that she didn't think she'd ever see me again when I left her to come home. I responded by suggesting we get married so that she could stay in the United States indefinitely. She went to the women's bathroom for what seemed like an hour to think it over, then came out and said she'd get married. Two days later we went to the judge in Cook County, Illinois, found witnesses in the hallway, and stood before the judge who made up vows like having me always mow the lawn and she always taking care of the house. It was ridiculous, but we had a marriage license. In fairness, I was wearing jeans with holes in the knees and she was wearing tie dye leggings (the couple after us was in formal wedding attire, so the judge was merely playing to his audience). While in Chicago, we were invited to Patrick's mom and dad's house for dinner. We went, and guess who else was there? Katie. Yes, my future wife, the first woman I ever made love with, the future mother of our children, the woman I was always meant to be with, was sitting at the very table with Kassandra and me. That was hard! I really, really tried to be present for Kassandra, to not let her feel like an outsider amongst my friends that were like family to me, and I think I succeeded, but I don't know.

What I do know, all these years later, is what a struggle my heart was having. We didn't tell anyone that we were married; she was a girlfriend as far as everyone knew, even Patrick. The next day we drove to Des Moines and ended up renting a farmhouse about ten miles to the west in the middle of nowhere. That was a mistake. Kassandra had nothing to do during the day while I was gone framing houses. We slept on an inflatable mattress. She had a birthday during that time and my mom gave her a present; she never opened it and insisted I take it back. She didn't think my mom liked her. She might have been right, but my mom was trying. Kassandra saw everything in black and white and once she got hold of a notion, it stuck like dogma to a zealot. We went to Denver to visit my fishing buddy, Scott. While there we had a great time. We saw Crosby, Stills and Nash at Red Rocks Amphitheater and drove over to Great Sand Dunes National Park.

Ultimately, Kassandra was miserable, which made my life miserable, so I said goodbye to my mom and dad and my framing pals, again, sold my '63 Ford pickup, and we moved back to Ireland.

We lived in Berlin twice for about three months during two winters. Thanks to Kassandra, I discovered the music of Tom Waits; she had many of his albums and I spent hours listening to what is probably the greatest gift she gave me. I cried the first time I heard "Kentucky Avenue," and I didn't realize the prescience of "Ruby's Arms." We lived one winter in a flat that was heated by hot water pipes that fed the apartment above us. During each stint in Berlin, I came down with an illness that, to this day, I have no idea what it was; it had me bed-ridden in the fetal position for about a fortnight each time.

I've never been so sick in my life, and now I attribute the strength of my amazing immune system to whatever it overcame in those two separate attacks. I fell in love with Turkish falafel. I was at once fascinated by Berlin and thrown off balance by the palpable undercurrent of violence and death. One day, as a woman approached me on the sidewalk, what I thought were sunglasses turned out to be two black eyes. I saw more hands and wrists in casts than I'd ever seen, and I walked by apartment buildings that smelled like someone was lying dead on the other side of a window. I was enthralled by the history while seeing things like the one remaining section of the Berlin Wall, the Brandenburg Gate, the Reichstag, Sanssouci in Potsdam, and the Pergamon Museum. I read "Lonesome Dove" aloud to Kassandra over a two-week period in the evening while she knitted us slippers. Mellowing out with hashish crumbled into hand-rolled Dutch tobacco cigarettes was a frequent pastime; I think they called it a spliff.

Each time we left the city the same way we entered, through the central bus station, destination Dublin.

During our final time together in Ireland, in the spring, summer and fall of 1994 and prior to the second Berlin experience, I bought a motorcycle. Holy crap was that fun! Kassandra and I had moved to Galway City where I could work with Glenn Gibson, a friend of hers from her pre-Tom Doolin days. Glenn, formerly a cook at the Doolin Cafe, had recently moved there to become a chef at the Athenry Golf Club. Athenry is a town a few miles to the east of Galway City, and the golf club lies between the two towns; Glenn's dad was a member. Long story short, Kassandra missed Doolin and the sea while I was enjoying the chef gig, so she moved back to the coast while I stayed on in a new place in Athenry I rented with Glenn. Basically, Kassandra and I were separated.

The motorcycle rides I took from Athenry to Doolin to visit Kassandra, through the Burren or along the coast road from Kinvarra past Fanore to her room at Petey Tierney's farmhouse were probably the best times I've ever had on any road anywhere. Riding a motorcycle in Ireland has its challenges, what with the weather and livestock and narrow roads, but my goodness was it ever fun! Working in the restaurant with Glenn was a hoot. Listening to Van Morrison and Bob Marley while serving up meals until the last members had finished their rounds in the long summer nights, then speeding into town before the pubs closed, me on my motorbike, Glenn in his Toyota, to drink a Guinness, often sitting outside on the stone windowsill at half past eleven, pints in hand watching the sky go dark. My nickname for Glenn was Cochise; he loved that name so much that he called me Cochise as well. Kassandra called me Liebster, so I called her Liebe. The somewhat sad fact is that I enjoyed being with the Apache warrior more than love.

My Alaskan fishing buddy, Scott McBurney, came to Ireland and visited us. The only time I heard him play the piano was one afternoon when the three of us wandered around Galway City on a pilgrimage disguised as a pub crawl to find a piano. We entered an open Catholic church where, based on years of observation and experience, I had a hunch we'd find a piano. We did, and he was amazing.

I had no idea that when Kassandra and I saw him off at the departure area of Shannon Airport, it would be the last time I'd ever see him. I can picture that moment even now, he in his black leather jacket and dark jeans, backpack over his shoulder, as he waved goodbye. He was on his way to Alaska to work on fishing vessels again. Scott had parlayed the experiences we shared into a lucrative position with a company that helped Russia, Poland and other former Soviet-controlled countries upgrade their fishing industry. A few months later, I got a long-distance phone call at the apartment Kassandra and I were renting in Athenry before we separated. The call was from Scott's sister in Denver to tell me that Scott was found dead on a fishing boat while working up on the Bering Sea. It would never be proved, but all signs led to Scott being murdered by resentful Eastern Europeans when he was promoted to a position above them while out at sea. He was found, bludgeoned, in the holding tank of a trawler, as improbable as it was tragic. It grieves me to this day, nearly 30 years later, to think of Scott's loss to his family, his friends, and the world that he touched; he was a beautiful soul.

 Imagine how I felt when I got that call. It was news that left me simultaneously numb with sorrow and stung with a sense of my own mortality. I'd had brushes with death, once or twice on a fishing boat no less. What was I doing with my life? Why was I still here? I was about to delve into those questions and stop drifting from them. It was the beginning of the end of my time with Kassandra and that longer spell I have named "The Forsaken Years." It just took several months for me to break myself away and commit to a higher love.

 Shortly after that phone call, Kassandra and I separated. As I've mentioned, we tried one last time to make it work in Berlin. But hell, if it didn't work in Ireland, where would it? So, I left her, not unlike the hero in that Tom Waits' song that I must have listened to a few dozen times since I'd met her, and him; she gave me Tom Waits, and I gave her "Ruby's Arms." For a brief period, we shared a simple life sprinkled with adventure and travel. Mostly, she gave me the knowledge that I was now capable of loving someone. I was coming to a place in my life where I loved who I was, and that person deserved protection. I was ready to give myself to another because I now knew that I wasn't going away in a week or a month or three years to try to find myself. Had I stayed with Kassandra, I would have lost myself.

    I saw Kassandra one last time, a few months after I left her in Berlin. She had moved back to Doolin, had even purchased a parcel of land, and she needed me to come back to go through the couple of boxes of things we had left behind when we both left the previous winter. Ted was now living full time in Doolin, so I stayed with him. I have no idea what possessions might have needed my attention; I think we both just needed closure since I departed without a goodbye.

    We took a walk to her property, and I can only wonder now, as I write this, if she ever built a home on the site. Later, we sat in McGann's Pub and listened to Ted and his friends play traditional music. When the pub closed, the same one wherein we met, we walked out together and stopped on the small bridge above the River Aille. There we stood in the middle of the quiet road where another kind of river, the one that carried our two lives in a sometimes turbulent, sometimes pure current, was about to sever and never join again. She asked me to come with her and spend the night in her bed. With thoughts of Katie in my heart and mind, I declined. It really was a painful moment for both of us, for there was a genuine tenderness we both felt for what we had meant to each other for a brief but intense stretch of time. When the moment became too much to bear, she did us both a favor. She turned and ran away. That was the last time I saw Kassandra.

14
Goodnight Dad

After the week at my dear friend Dan's house in Big Rapids, I boarded an Indian Trails bus to Chicago. I could have stayed in the Windy City, shacked up with a friend while I found an apartment and a job, but I wanted to see my mom and dad. I boarded the next bus for home.

My mom and dad were always willing and happy to take me in after any adventure, without judgment, for as long as I needed to get my bearings or earn some money. Oh, my dad might say something like, "Why don't you use that teaching degree and get a job here?" Or he'd ask me if I wanted to take over his sales territory; he couldn't help it. They were fair suggestions, but not ones that I cared to entertain, and we mostly left it at that.

I suppose there are parents among those who may read these lines some day and think to themselves, "When my child leaves the home, they need to understand that there is no coming back and living in the basement." I suppose there were neighbors of my mom and dad that considered me a bit of a drifter, and lazy, to be 33 and single (Kassandra and I never told anyone we had been married by a justice of the peace in Cook County, not even my mom and dad), living with my parents, who should not be enabling a young man to come and go as he pleases.

Truth is, I never needed to move back in and stay with my mom and dad from time to time. I never in my life had a problem finding a job and a place to live. On the contrary, I wanted to stay with my mom and dad. I loved them dearly and I didn't care what the neighbors thought of me, or them. I loved getting up before dawn, making coffee, and reading until my folks came downstairs. Mom's home cooking sure didn't hurt matters. And at the end of the day, I was their son.

My mom loved cooking for her boy, even when her boy was a man. It gave my mom great joy to have me home. My dad, on the other hand, struggled with my presence to a degree simply because he, a true child of the Great Depression, struggled with just about every aspect of how I lived my life, how different it was to anything he experienced or imagined. Indeed, my dad lived in that house for just over 30 years, paid off the mortgage and worked, literally, until the day he died, which I'm slowly getting to.

You see, I also felt indebted to my mom and dad. I can't speak for every person that was adopted, but I know that I felt I owed them so much more than phone calls, letters, and the odd long weekend visit here and there. It's an obligation I harbored from those earliest days of knowing. It's an understanding of the commitment they made to me the day they chose me and honored every day of my life. It's the deepest sense of gratitude I own. It's why I couldn't go to Ireland without first taking them with me, and the reason why I was sleeping on the daybed in their basement in February 1995.

And I suppose there are those among us who are thinking, "The best way to show your parents gratitude is to make something of your life, be independent, strong. Not by showing up at their door with a meager bank account, no car to get you to your job at the casino, and no plan for where you'll be in six months."

To that I would say, "I agree with you!" The last thing I want for my two sons, each in their early twenties, is to come home to live for anything more than a week or ten days. But if they do, I will welcome them with love and compassion, without judgment, unconditionally, for as long as they need to be with Katie and me. Not because I've been there and done that. Simply because I am their dad and I love them. My days of tough love with my sons are behind me. I no longer need to throw televisions off the back deck or abandon shopping carts in the middle of the aisle or keep their cell phones out of their bedroom at night or deprive them of some other perceived must have or must do. I only need to be there for them no matter what. Like my mom and dad were for me.

"Wait! Did you say you were working at a casino?"

"Yeah, I was working at a casino. Fight me!"

I could have just said I had a job with all the bells and whistles and left it at that. But no, I literally worked as a slot attendant in a casino attached to a horse track called Prairie Meadows, unclogging machines, paying off jackpots, keeping my section tidy, and annoying my supervisors by ignoring walkie talkie protocols.

I worked the 3-11 p.m. shift. The only person I really connected with was a retired over-the-road trucker named James with more stories than a small-town library. We are friends to this day. The rest was a mostly twenty-something group that I'd sometimes go sing karaoke with at a local bar after a shift, myself the "old man" in the crowd.

My go-to song was Van Morrison's "Brown Eyed Girl," which is a little ironic. After an evening of some drinking and song, and a few days after I spontaneously bought a necklace from the casino gift shop with tip money which another young slot attendant named Carla had told me in passing that she had seen and liked and then gave her with no intention of a return of any pleasant pleasantry other than a smile and thank you, I happened to find myself making love in the green grass with a brown eyed girl. Only it wasn't a stadium, it was behind my mom and dad's house where the swing set used to stand. Working at a racetrack and casino must have rubbed off on her because she rode me like a jockey, spent the night on the family room sofa, and left the next morning very early.

I don't like to be irreverent when it comes to intimate relations, but I couldn't resist.

I worked that job until July 1995. I'll always remember what year that was because it was the year Van Morrison's album "Days Like This" was released. I listened to that CD almost every day on my way to work. I'll always remember it was July because it was the month my dad died. He was buried on my birthday.

I learned several years later that Monday is the most frequent day of the week for men to have a heart attack. Such was the case for my dad.

I had been staying at my friend's apartment in town while he was away with his girlfriend on a cruise. I had the use of his car while he was gone. My parents and sister knew where I was, no big deal.

The phone rang that morning. I answered it. It was my mom telling me to come home because dad wasn't feeling well and she was worried. He had gone about his usual Monday morning pre-work routine and had left for the day to make sales calls. He got as far as the gas station where he filled the tank but wasn't feeling great. He decided he'd return home and rest a bit. He walked in the door, which in and of itself was enough to set my mom to worrying. He told her he wasn't feeling well and went into the family room to rest in his favorite chair. My mom brought him the glass of water he had asked for and then called me. Sometime shortly after we hung up, she heard a gasp from the family room; her husband was having a heart attack. She called 911 and the paramedics were there working on him when I arrived. I stood at the top of the stairs and watched them try to revive him. Within minutes, they put him on a stretcher, told my mom they were taking him to the hospital and instructed us to follow. I held the storm door as they carried him out and away, ostensibly still working on him, but I knew he had died. Paramedics aren't paid to break the news to loved ones.

Almost all ordinary men and women are great, simply being human makes them so. The extraordinary ones, the great thinkers and artists and innovators, leaders, and heroes, although perhaps special and no doubt gifted, are no greater than my dad. You and I know that a lot of extraordinary men get there on the backs of others. My dad was a man who was born the oldest of a brood of children to a first generation Irish-American couple on Chicago's northside. He took a job as a boy shoveling manure out of a stable when the Depression hit to help support the family, and he held a job every day, week, month, and year of his life after that, save the years he spent serving his country in WWII. He and my mom bought a house in 1964 and made it a home. He was a solitary man, often gone from home a week at a time making sales calls, enabling my sometimes-lonely mom to joyfully stay at home and raise their kids. He only got paid when he made a sale, without a salary or benefits, strictly on commission, and he provided for us all; and if you don't mind me saying so, that takes tremendous skill and courage and perseverance and strength and will and balls the size of the bells on the church he attended and ushered at every Sunday of his life when he wasn't out of town on a vacation that wasn't paid for by his company. Nobody gave my dad a hand up, no one fought his battles for him, he stepped on no one. He never missed a payment on the thirty-year mortgage he paid off less than a year before he died. He taught me how to grill. He didn't laugh often, but when he did it was a downright guffaw and his belly shook. His life and mine are almost opposites, but because I have also lived an ordinary life, because I've been a father and felt a father's love, I can feel great myself. I'm a bona fide giant thanks to him.

When I was a boy, I used to give my dad a kiss and tell him goodnight before I went to bed. He was usually sitting in his favorite chair watching TV, sometimes nodding off to sleep. I distinctly remember getting to the age where I no longer wanted to give him a kiss, I just wanted to say goodnight, and I labored for weeks trying to get up the nerve to tell him I thought I was too old to be kissing my dad goodnight. Finally, one evening I walked down the stairs into the family room where my dad sat, perhaps watching "Mannix" or some other of the detective shows he so enjoyed. From the bottom of the stairs, I said, "Goodnight, dad." After a brief pause, he replied, "Goodnight, son." That was it. I turned around and went to my room feeling kind of like I had hurt his feelings.

If I knew then what I know now, it would have gone something like this:

As I walked down the stairs, I would have said, "Dad, I'm coming to say goodnight but I think I'm getting too old to kiss you goodnight anymore. Is that okay?"

Projecting a little of my own sentiment into the situation, my dad would have paused for a moment to consider that something he truly cherished, and that both of us probably took for granted, was soon to go away forever with hardly a warning.

But then, as I stood at the bottom of the stairs for what seemed like minutes waiting for my dad to say something, it would occur to me that in life we rarely get the opportunity to grasp when something is going to happen for the last time, and wouldn't it be a swell gift to both of us if we knew ahead of time that there would be one final goodnight kiss. So, before my dad could say, "That's all right son, goodnight." I would say:

"Actually, dad, can I have a hug? You mean the world to me."

Dad would get out of his chair and we'd hug. Then I'd remember my favorite song on the Louis Armstrong album I might have played that day on the '50s era Magnavox console in the living room, "A Kiss to Build a Dream On." I'd kiss my dad on the cheek, say goodnight, and run off to bed.

"Give me a kiss before you leave me
And my imagination will feed my hungry heart
Leave me one thing before we part
A kiss to build a dream on."

15
Out of the Ashes

I figured I was finished writing about Kassandra, but I just had a thought as I re-read what I had written at the end of the last chapter, triggered by the reality of how most times we never know that something is going to happen for the last time. Specifically, I'm thinking of the moment on the bridge that last night I saw Kassandra when she asked me to spend the night with her. I always believed that she was merely interested in trying to moor a ship that was sailing away. I knew then that it was futile. But what if all she wanted was the chance to be together one last time, knowing it would be the last time, and giving the moment the tenderness it probably deserved.

I'll likely never know Kassandra's motive. But I do believe with a great amount of certainty that, even if I had the maturity back then to consider the beauty of her wanting the heightened experience which full awareness of closure brings, I still would have declined her offer.

I didn't need one last day of work at the casino to experience more fully how it would feel to walk away from the job, or to etch into my brain the memories of a day in the life of a slot machine attendant, to let me sear the sounds of bells and sirens into my brain, to let me bask in the wafts of secondhand smoke, to let me witness the hope written on a face when the first coin is kissed and the despair when the last coin vanishes.

There was no one I needed to say goodbye to.

And so, on the first day back after we buried my dad on my 34th birthday, I went into work and quit my job. My boss really was a good dude. He told me that I could take as much time off as I needed, that he understood how difficult it is to lose a father and maybe I needn't be so quick to make decisions like quitting a job when my heart is so heavy with grief.

Truth be told, it wasn't a quick decision. I was getting ready to quit before my dad died and making plans to move back to Chicago. I had a place to stay; an actor friend of an actor friend had an empty bedroom in his two-bedroom, north side apartment that he was thrilled to offer me to ease his rent. I had a job; Patrick Kelly's brother, Mike, started his own construction company and was thrilled to hire me on as a carpenter/laborer.

I know, moving away doesn't seem like a very loving thing for a son to do to his mom in the immediate wake of her husband of 46 years' death. On the surface, it seems damn cold. Let me briefly explain.

My older sister and her husband were either divorced or soon to be divorced, and they leaned heavily on my mom to care for their three beautiful young daughters; my mom was an angel. My younger sister was also around; she leaned heavily on my mom for emotional support and vice versa. It was all way too much drama for me. I like my drama on the page, stage, and screen, not in a relationship, family or otherwise. I mean, I won't go so far as to infer that life in mom's house was like living in Edinburgh during the Fringe Festival, but let's just say my sisters and mom could juggle. I loaded up my big green duffle bag, which was just a few pounds lighter than the guilt I was suppressing over leaving mom. I snagged my tool belt and bucket, a few select hand tools from my dad's toolbox in his office (which I devotedly keep on my workbench in the garage), and boarded a Greyhound bound for Chicago.

16
7,500 Bowls of Cereal

There is a very kind woman in town named Tiffany who, through her work, has access to adoption files at our local Catholic Charities office. Because of Tiffany's efforts, I've learned quite a bit about Rita's life in the weeks and months leading up to my birth. In a letter that she wrote to a priest in Des Moines prior to her leaving Philadelphia, she wrote, "I am due July 30 and I'll be going to Mercy Hospital to have my baby. It's so difficult to make definite plans when I don't really know what to do, except pray that my parents, sisters, and brother never find out why I'm really leaving Philadelphia, pray that I keep my good spirits and cheerfulness and that the baby is going to be all right. Whatever sacrifices I have to make, I'll make. It will be worth it."

In that same letter, Rita petitions the priest to help her land a nursing job at the very hospital where I was born because "I'm afraid of what boredom could do to me."

All this to say that my birth mother cared for me the best she could. She worked as a nurse right up until my birth, thus staving off the dreaded boredom and, I believe, keeping her good spirits and cheerfulness.

What is a nurse if not compassionate and caring? With that in mind, I imagine the moments after my birth when I was placed in Rita's arms for the first time, perhaps the only time. No doubt she felt tremendous relief that her pregnancy was complete and that she was now on the threshold of wherever she saw her life going.

With a healthy, beautiful boy in her arms, she must have had tender words to say to me, undoubtedly rooted in the faith she had and the hope that the care she had given me for nine months would be continued and carried out for a lifetime. I believe she told me that she wished me a lifetime of love.

Rita's wish began when I was placed with my mom and dad. Her wish came true when Katie accepted my love for the second time. Dear, darling, beautiful Katie. There is not a word that alights more wonderfully and tenderly on my heart than Katie…Katie…Katie.

With a nice apartment to live in and a job in hand, I hit the ground running when I got to Chicago. "The Forsaken Years" were behind me, those amazing experiences mingled with moments of despair. I could say to Mr. Waits that, at least in my case, when the devils are exorcized, the angels remain. Maybe a therapist could have saved me a lot of time and mileage, but I rather like the way I came to like myself, accept myself, and prepare myself to love; it probably cost me about the same. To borrow a phrase from James Joyce, if I may be so bold, I had "forged in the smithy of my soul" a love of self and a joy in life. With those two arrows in my quiver, I was finally ready to love a woman.

Katie was dating another guy! Another guy with a (gasp) career! The dude led the mayor's Office of Special Events, or something like that. Backstage passes, VIP tickets, access, his own car, you get the picture. I was 34, sleeping on an inflatable mattress in a fellow actor's spare bedroom and borrowing his bicycle. All my possessions could have fit in the trunk of that dude's car.

What chance did I have?

Oh, how fortunate it was for me that Katie favored toast over toasts, imagination over image, potential over potency, care over career, and music over musing. Not everyone does.

Because the journey is most often more magnificent than the individual ports of call, I'm going to spare you, fair reader, the deep dive into the daily joys of cruising on the Courtship Katie, where nearly every day began with a thought of her, and where many days ended in a bed beside her, and in between lived a man enabled to be, simply, himself. I didn't have to pretend to be anything or anyone. I didn't have to worry if I was good enough. I didn't have to censor what I said or wonder how it would be taken. I was free to love.

I'd like to think that Katie felt the same. I didn't judge her. I didn't burden her with expectations or demands, and I didn't feel diminished or threatened by her success.

In short, neither of us had to settle for a lesser version of ourselves when we were together. I think that is one of the keys to a lasting love, for it has been a constant tenet of our relationship since the day we reunited in early autumn 1995.

I remember knowing that Katie was planning to be at the performance of the play I was going to attend that evening at the theater company where I was soon to become an ensemble member, American Blues. She was seated away from me to my left with her friend, Colleen Kelly.

Katie was so beautiful, so pretty that night at the theater. She had come from work, dressed to the nines.

Seriously, if I boarded a CTA bus heading downtown and she was sitting there on her way to work, myself going to some construction job or perhaps to an audition for some role or voiceover, not knowing her I would take one look and probably say to myself, "Don't even think about it."

As it was, we talked at intermission. After the play, I had the honor of walking her home to her apartment about six blocks from the theater. Neither one of us can recall if I spent the night, and it really doesn't matter. What is truly meaningful is that it was the rebirth of our life together.

In between then and our wedding two years later, there were concerts and plays and dinners and trips to our hometown. Katie took a three-week vacation to trek in the Himalayas of Nepal, during which time I wrote her a letter every day. As letters go, it was a tome and a genuine testament to my love for her. After that, I bought an engagement ring from a jeweler in Des Moines and he shipped it to me when it was done. I picked it up at the post office and walked back to the apartment we now shared with it stashed in the nether reaches of my skivvies.

I had the ring in my possession when we went to her parents' house for Thanksgiving in 1996. It was the coldest meal I think I've ever eaten; her dad wouldn't even look at me when he learned his 36-year-old daughter and I were living together. I couldn't ask for her hand, let alone tell him that I was going to propose in a little over a week in New York City when I accompanied Katie on a business trip. That proposal happened on December 7.

I carried the ring all day in the inside breast pocket of my dad's hand-me-down leather coat as we walked the city. I obtained the barely worn coat after he passed. I remember constantly tapping my chest to make sure it was still there. I finally couldn't stand the wait and suspense any longer, so when we ducked into the Old Town Bar just off Park Avenue on E. 18th Street for a beer in the late afternoon, I presented the ring, a one carat stone in a platinum setting, and asked Katie if she'd marry me. She said yes, but in true Katie fashion she asked if we could go to a place she knew from previous travels, the Royalton Hotel, and have a glass of champagne under the chandeliers. I put the ring back in my coat and we went to the hotel. We sat on a sofa together under the lights and ordered champagne. When the flutes arrived, I produced the ring and reenacted the proposal. Katie knew what she was doing. Under the chandeliers, her ring sparkled and shone like, well, like the name she gave it: The Beacon.

During our honeymoon, we bought three cereal bowls from a potter's studio. Perhaps they weren't intended to be "cereal" bowls, but that's what I used them for. I've taken my cereal from one of them nearly every day of my married life that wasn't called holiday or Sunday. Today, 25+ years after that lovely week on Martha's Vineyard, there is one bowl remaining, with a significant chip gone from the rim and significant portions of the glaze gone from the bottom of the bowl. None of the bowls ever saw the inside of a dishwasher.

It is important to say that there is tremendous intention surrounding what could arguably be considered the most mundane task of my married life: pouring my cereal, eating my cereal, and cleaning the bowl.

Intention. It is how that bowl survives in its everyday place atop the soup bowls in the cabinet and while drying on the towel beside the sink amidst thugs like pans, knives, cutting boards and coffee mugs. It is also how love and marriage survive and thrive, intention.

Believe me, when there were three bowls, there was a lot less intention. It's only when I was down to my last fragile bowl that things got intentional. I am so grateful to have earned a bit of wisdom, that, having lived most of my life up to then with a chip on my own rim, I had the will to live what I had learned and understood what it meant to take care. I knew then what I know now, and isn't it amazing to be able to say that? To be able to live with and love Katie every day for the rest of my life, to survive change and grow, to understand disappointments, to listen, to be present, all I really had to do was care.

And none of this would have been possible had Katie not been the greatest enabler of my life. What do I mean by that? Simply put, Katie makes the best margarita I've ever tasted and is a fantastic mixologist.

Although what I just wrote is true, it's not what makes her my enabler. Because of Katie, I have been able to wake up every morning of my married life in love, with her, with myself, free to create or fail or dream or play, to never feel not good enough or strong enough or rich enough. What a blessing that is, she is.

In my weakest moments, when I look around at my peers and see what they're driving or wearing or winning or earning, I wallow in self-pity and doubt for about ten seconds. Then I lift myself up by my belt and neck, press myself against the coat hooks of my mind and say, "Knock that shit off!"

I am so grateful that she saw enough of what could be me during "The Forsaken Years" that she was present when I was finally ready and able to be me.

All that being said, our marriage probably would have ended after about eight years if Katie had insisted that I keep hanging those fickle, fucking, lying, cheating, ass-clown crappers called Christmas lights on our trees and bushes outside with numb fingers pulling and prying and testing bulbs that worked before I strung them and somehow failed when they contacted dormant organic matter. After a few seasons of folly amidst the holly, I slammed my size twelve boot down hard, threw my gloves into the coat closet and said, "Sweetheart, honey, would you mind if I don't do the lights this year? I'll hold the ladder for you and I'll love you forever!"

Katie does the lights now and I hold the ladder. She does it because it makes her happy and rolls her eyes when we're driving anywhere in November and December past some house where a man is stringing lights outside and I say, "Poor bastard." Perhaps he's a kinder, more loving man who strings those lights because it makes his bride happy. All I can say is that it's good to know your limits.

17
Touched

Life since my marriage to Katie more than 25 years ago feels like one event. The connective tissue from our wedding day to our life now, and the focus I've maintained through it all, makes it seem more like a moment than a memory. I believe it is that connective tissue which has enabled us to feel a closeness to our sons, now in their early 20s, residing more than one thousand miles from our home.

The expression, "That seems like another lifetime ago," is a common one. It's how I feel about my life pre-Katie and why writing about it flowed pretty easily; I could have written it in the third person. It's as if everything I wrote up to now is akin to me performing on stage, bringing another character to life, naturally. What's coming next suddenly feels very personal and it scares me, as if everything I'm about to write is my script for a TED Talk about marriage and fatherhood to a conference of cynics, psychoanalysts, writers, lovers, and pre-80's Catholic school English teachers.

Well, what can I do, quit now? Walk away? Take a bike ride?

That old, ridiculous advice I think I was given in a high school speech class about imagining one's audience as naked to ease the anxiety doesn't work when writing. If anyone reading this is naked… actually, cool. I guess we're both letting it all hang out.

I probably saw my mom and dad kiss more than once, but once is all I remember, when they renewed their wedding vows on their 25th anniversary. I was 12. I don't recall them kissing when my dad went to work in the morning or returned from a week on the road, kissing good night or good morning, holding hands, hugging, dancing in the kitchen or at a cousin's wedding (they did dance at my sisters' weddings), or cuddling on a sofa. There was no intimacy, at least in view of their kids. I was kind of paying attention.

I am certainly not trying to throw them under the bus or judge their love. I have no interest in any of that. However, parents are role models, and when it came to showing affection, I knew precisely how I didn't want to be thought of as a husband, to Katie or our boys.

Affection seems to be something that we innately recognize the instant we are born. My own intuition tells me that one's willingness to give or receive true affection stems largely from the patterns experienced from birth through adolescence. I must have received enough of it as a child to grasp its importance as a parent.

At the end of the day, being affectionate is a choice we make. (It's a darn fine one at the beginning of the day as well.) It is not something that is automatic or lacking depending on how we're raised and what we experience growing up. Which makes me wonder if there is a marker for affection in our DNA, or markers that trigger how we respond to signs of affection. Since I'm the only member of this case study and based on the understanding I have of the scientific process learned in advanced chemistry when I was sixteen, I'm going to say yes to affection and thank you, Rita, for being so dominant.

The question I ask myself is how I learned its importance in an adult relationship. Not from watching my parents or my friend's parents or my aunts and uncles, and not in a book. I think the answer lies in how the simplest human touch made me feel. I remember sitting in the stands of the gymnasium during a high school assembly or the seats in an auditorium, next to a girl, and if her arm brushed up against mine in the slightest way it toppled whatever else was on my mind at the time. Even if it was a guy, if he wasn't an ass, I wouldn't move my arm or knee. Even now, on an airplane for example, if a stranger's arm or shoulder or knee comes to rest against mine a little, I'm okay with it. It goes beyond mere hormonal charge to something elemental: human touch. It's that simple. Being open to touch helps. The way I responded to examples of it as I grew older told me how deeply I cared for it in my relationships, both as something to give and receive. I know how I feel about someone by the way I react to their touch, and by my willingness to touch them. That being said, if you're a dude in an aisle or window seat and you are taking up my middle seat armrest as well, do not touch me, fucker!

The most heartfelt words might fail to land without an accompanying touch. And at some point in your life, when all your lover wants to do is read, a touch will speak volumes from you.

Touch with Katie is blissful in all its manifestations, and in its sweetest, purest, and most intense sharing it led to three pregnancies and two births.

Although it's not unusual for a first pregnancy to end in a miscarriage, for Katie and me, and I imagine for most couples trying to create a baby, it was a moment of deep sadness. For a woman, there is the sorrow, but with it come feelings of despair and inadequacy. And since the miscarriage often comes before any announcement is made to family and friends, there is the additional burden of bearing the sorrow alone.

I sensed all this that afternoon when I met Katie at the doctor's office. There were no words to console her. There was nothing to do but hold her and listen. Touch her. I think that words are nice in a situation like this, that it's possible to convey compassion, love and understanding. But I really believe that only touch can soothe the deepest hurts that come when the spark of life within a woman goes dark. And time. And a successful pregnancy.

It was later that I told her of my mom's five miscarriages. And it's only now, in the context of writing a memoir inspired by my own birth mother's story and my own adoption, that I've gained an insight into why my mom felt compelled to tell me about her miscarriages so often. I'll never know for sure, but I think it was my mom's way of talking about my adoption without talking about my adoption. What other reason would my mom have for telling me, so many times that it is seared into my memory, than to let me know how badly she wanted a baby and how precious I was to her, her only son, her chosen one.

How different my life would have been had she not had those miscarriages. Five failed pregnancies led to my beautiful placement with my mom and dad. From a depth of great sorrow flowed a warm spring of tremendous love and caring and commitment....to me.

And it almost goes without saying that if Katie and I did not suffer that initial miscarriage, our sons would not be with us today. Yes, things turned out rather well. Katie got pregnant again quickly and our first son was born in March 1999, with his brother following in August 2000.

18
Houses and Homes

Katie and I had a huge advantage heading into married life. Her dad and grandpa had set aside a fund for her and her two sisters that would enable them to purchase a starter home when the time came. And so it was that we were able to buy an 1890's era Marshall Field row house in Chicago's Bucktown neighborhood and have no debt, no mortgage and little worry. What a gift! We immediately set about a full-blown gut rehab and turned it into a little two bedroom, two-and-a-half bath gem by the time Seamus was born. I served as the contractor on the remodel and did a ton of the work in the off hours of working construction and performing in the odd play in town. A job of that magnitude (we tore off the entire back of the house and added on) had its stresses and challenges to be sure, but Katie was patient, resilient and very happily pregnant. We lived in the basement amidst the dust and debris of renovation. Katie nurtured the life inside her, all the while going to work in the day and making all kinds of design and decorating decisions in the evenings and weekends, blissfully feathering the nest for our first child.

All this to say that when our son was born, we were ready. The dream we had envisioned for our life was being realized in all its beauty, without fear and with deep appreciation for the moment and the life and love we had. Yes, Katie had some of the doubt and worry that many first-time mothers experience, but we had each other. And what a beautiful mother Katie was! And still is!

※

When I wrote earlier about how Katie is the great enabler of my life, this is what I was trying to say: she made me a dad.

At the risk of sounding pompous, fatherhood is what I think I was put on this earth to do, and everything I'd done and experienced prepared me for that day in March 1999. Being born an orphan, being loved unconditionally by my mom and dad, yearning for a spiritual home, longing for knowledge of a blood relation, and pretty much being a kid at heart all added up to the thrill and ease I felt when our son was born. Lying in the hospital bed with Katie, our newborn baby in our arms, I knew exactly what I had to do. Don't we all? The instruction manual unfolds in our hearts as intuition and love words and songs and wisdom. All we must do is listen.

※

Thus, on March 24, 1999, I became a stay-at-home dad!

You see, one of the things Katie and I felt strongly about, from the beginning, was that if we were fortunate enough to have children, one of us would stay home; there would be no day care. And this is not a slam on day care; the truth is that many parents simply don't have an option. If anything, it's a slam on a society that has evolved into one that demands two medium incomes to manage a household healthfully when it used to be handled with one. And I won't judge parents who opt for day care yet possess the means to do otherwise; some of the dearest friends I love chose day care. We all must do what works for us. I'm just grateful I had a choice, even though there was no choice to make. Becoming a stay-at-home dad was the role of a lifetime.

(If I were going to take a swing at day care, it would go something like this: A society gets what it deserves when it allows its representatives in government to subsidize day care expenses with tax deductions then laments the breakdown of the family. If day care is really the best option for a family, why does it feel like hell the first time the child is dropped off? A question to ponder: Why did day care providers proliferate after Roe v. Wade? Shouldn't there have been less demand? This is all an example of a type of writing exercise I call "writing as a rehearsal actor," where the director of the "play," aka the editor in my head, says, "Okay, I asked you to take the character to a dark place to see what we discover, but I've seen enough. There may be a shred of truth in there, but it's not true to the character. It doesn't move the story in a meaningful way and you're going to piss off a lot of our audience.")

It was a no-brainer who would stay home in our family. Katie earned at least three times more in salary and bonuses than what I made bending nails while working construction, and it amounted to more than enough for us to live very comfortably; you know, shop at Whole Foods and buy the odd baby outfit at the Oilily Outlet Store in Michigan.

No, it was so much more than that!

Truth be told, being a stay-at-home dad was the sweetest gig in the world and, other than voiceover work, the easiest job I ever had. I had no career to sacrifice to stay at home with the boys. I learned early on that acting was never going to be a career for me, it was simply something I really liked to do and could do well. Anymore, if I fantasize about being nominated for an acting award, it's only so that I could walk the red carpet with Katie by my side wearing a designer dress and to accept the award on her behalf because everything I am and everything I have is because of her love. Seriously. Everything.

Katie provided everything for me and our two boys. I was up playing with the boys while Katie got ready for work. I was often at the park while Katie drove 45 minutes or more in Chicago traffic to get to her office. I probably helped my boys learn to walk or ride a bike while Katie was being reduced to tears by some hardass bitch of a client. Many times, I eked out an extra twenty minutes of nap time by lying down stealthily on the sofa with a sleepy baby on my chest after carefully lifting him out of his crib while Katie gave a presentation to clients looking at their cell phones. I got to build forts while Katie broke through walls, and we all got to be there when Katie got home, every day. What a woman! Katie is a thousand times tougher than I ever was or will be. My boys and I are living proof of how a man can soar with a woman's love.

And this is important: Yes, I was nurturing. I was patient. I tried to teach and guide. I could happily cook and clean and run errands (when traffic was light). I harbored no resentment. I was devoted. But wanting or expecting praise and thanks and credit for being those things for my own children would be like a bee wanting tribute from the flowers.

Katie is all those things, and then some! In addition to being an amazing provider, she is an amazing wife and mom. Motherhood is not something she sacrificed on the altar of her career. She did it all! If I can boast for a moment, I'm proud that I played a part in letting her be Katie. We rarely took the other for granted, and if either of us had a moment when we doubted our value or purpose or direction, we were there with heartfelt reminders of what we were creating. Often, at the end of a day of mundane tasks and just being present in our boys' lives, all it took was hearing Katie sing to them as they drifted off to sleep to know that everything was right in the world.

※

With another baby on the way, we sold the row house and moved to a larger home on North Pontchartrain Boulevard in the Wildwood neighborhood on Chicago's far northwest side. Life there was as good as it gets in a big city, in a neighborhood with interesting architecture, railroad tracks, a firehouse, a public library, and a shop with a wooden Indian out front. There was easy access to bicycle and walking trails, and we were a stroller or wagon ride away from two great playgrounds with nary a single used condom in sight by the curb! And we cut Katie's commute in half.

Although every move we made was in a positive effort to make life better for our family, there was always a bit of a dark cloud in the current situation that made the move all the easier. For example, while Katie loved that rowhouse on Leavitt and we poured enormous sweat equity into making it a home, it all paid off in the end because it enabled us to afford the house where we moved. But we might have stayed a little longer if we didn't have a thoughtless rowhouse neighbor (he shared a wall with us) who used his back yard as a dumpster that attracted varmints which infested our home, and the aforementioned condoms that I suspect came from the neighbors across the street that resented our invasion of their neighborhood, and the eastern European nannies that used the park as their ashtray and whose butts would end up in my son's hands if I wasn't paying attention. These things ate away at me.

※

At 7:45 a.m. Central time on September 11, 2001, I was already at the park with the boys when the first plane hit the north tower. A woman came up to me and asked if I'd heard about the plane that crashed into the building in New York City. I hadn't. It was so early on that she didn't know it was a terrorist attack. She made out like it was a commuter plane or something. We kept playing.

Graham was two weeks past his first birthday and was already walking. I remember spending most of my time that morning keeping him from falling off the swinging bridge that his brother was playing on. At some point, I sensed that something was amiss. I don't recall noticing at the time that there were no airplanes flying in the sky, an oddity on the northwest side of Chicago. Maybe it registered in my subconscious. I do recall noticing that we were the only ones at the park. Whatever the reason, I rounded up the boys and we headed home, much sooner than we would have.

I turned on the TV and watched in horror while the boys played and ran through the house. It's hard to believe that was more than 21 years ago.

We left North Pontchartrain Boulevard a few weeks before our second son, Graham, turned two. (By the way, to call North Pontchartrain a boulevard is a stretch. With no curbs, it may be the shortest street in the city.) My mom had been diagnosed with colon cancer and was starting treatments, Katie's job paid her ridiculous money but she wasn't happy, and the attack on the World Trade Center left us craving a simpler life. The ultimate silver lining, aside from being close to my mom as she fought in vain for her life for five months, was that we lived a few blocks away from Katie's mom and dad. They were a tremendous factor in our decision to move back to our hometown, to be closer to the boys' grandparents, Nana and Papa.

The time that Katie and I and our two sons have been blessed to share with Terry and Jim Hammer (Nana and Papa) over the last 20+ years is the singular reason why we can say that moving back to Des Moines was the greatest thing we ever did as parents and as a family. Everything else we did, we could have done anywhere, but the thought of having done anything anywhere but here makes me sad to even consider. Now, as they dance their graceful dance on each side of ninety years, we all have the thrill and honor to play in their band every day and enjoy the music together.

One of the benefits of writing a memoir is the revelations that come from deep meditations on past events, the players and the lessons learned. One of those hit me hard this morning when, after days of contemplation (years, really), I sat down to write of my mom's passing.

The saddest meal I've ever eaten was the family Christmas dinner at my mom's house, about a month before she died. It was sad at the time, even more so now. I rarely visit the memory but this morning it decided to visit me.

As the memory was settling in on the sofa inside my mind, the usual images piled out of a day bag as if to say, "Hold on, we've got a little surprise for you."

I waited as mom, still weakened and tired from the chemo and radiation treatments, adjusted her wig at the head of the dining room table nearest the kitchen. I took in all the familiar objects in the '50's era breakfront, beyond where Ray McHenry used to sit, that hadn't moved in forty years. I gazed over at where my dad used to sit and still can't recall who had the cheek to sit there, six plus years after he last said grace. I choked back tears as my sister brought out the store-bought dinner in take-out containers, thinking about all the feasts that my mom put on that table over the years. And that's when, for the first time, guilt stepped out of the bag and slapped me in the face. "Surprise!"

"You could have made that meal a feast," it went on. "You knew how to cook. She taught you! You knew she was worn down! All you had to do was show up and be there for her like she was for you every time you needed her, every time! How happy would that have made your mom to have you cooking in her kitchen, playing music, singing, laughing, your sons running around her house filling it with joy? And don't blame it on your sister or the chaos that reigned in that house at the time. You lived in an almost half-million-dollar house and could have served twenty-five people in your kitchen."

And that's why I'm sitting here with tears running down my cheeks, the screen blurry, trying to forgive and understand and learn, maybe share a thing or two.

All I can say is that I didn't know. I didn't know it was mom's last Christmas. We all thought she was cancer free. We didn't know that the cancer had spread to her brain and was spreading quickly. But she knew. She kept it to herself. How do I know this?

In the end, mom wasn't eating, was nauseous, dehydrated. Not knowing what else to do, my younger sister Mary and I decided to check her into the hospital so she could get some fluids. I came over to the house and Mary had told mom what we were planning. She tried to fight us; she fought as hard as she could not to go, but we thought we knew best. We called the ambulance. By the time they arrived, mom had removed her rings from her fingers and laid them on the bedside table behind the untouched water glass. None of us saw them there, but twenty-four hours later, when we came home to pick out a dress for mom to be buried in, I saw them. She knew she wasn't coming home.

Mom most likely would have died in her sleep that night in her own bed had we not had her moved to the hospital. She went into cardiac arrest the following morning and I had to call off the nurses who were pounding on her chest and pleading with me to either pursue extraordinary measures to resuscitate or let her go. I let her go.

What about the guilt? I'm going to let it go, too. It came, it laid its heavy words on my heart, I listened, and I've decided to not let it haunt me. I'll let it teach me what it needs to teach. I'll cherish each visit with Katie's folks, for example. I know that the man I was twenty years ago wasn't ready for his mom to die. I couldn't see it, despite the cancer and the chemo. Life without

Moira? Of course, there will be another Christmas dinner with her.

Perhaps it's easy to let the guilt go because the best version of myself came into being the day I was placed in my mom's arms for the first time, and I wasn't ready to live in a world where those arms were gone.

And because I can see my mom at that table twenty years ago, looking at her grandchildren for what turned out to be one of the last times in her life, I know she had to be seeing the dream she had of my life passing before her eyes as brightly as her own was dimming, and I owe it to her to never let guilt stand in the way of her love.

Love the ones you're with. Forgive the one you're with, yourself.

When we moved back to Iowa, the plan was to find a rental house while we took our time looking for a home. We landed in a farmhouse in Cumming, about ten miles south of Des Moines. No sooner than we were coming, we were going. We made it three months in that drafty old farmhouse surrounded by hawks and horizons and barns and fields, where we had to walk to the post office and get our mail from P.O. Box 69! (When offered a choice by the postmaster, I couldn't resist the chance to send mail to my buddies with the return address in Cumming, Iowa, and told her that 69 was a jersey number in high school. It wasn't my number, but it was a number.) The last straw was when the mice found Katie's chocolate in her bedside table. Those were dark days for Katie, regardless of the beauty of the place and the fun we had with the boys. It was too much too soon for a lady that loved the city she left and had no job for really the first time in her professional life. It wasn't fair, she was truly in despair, and we got out of there just in time for the holidays. We don't talk about it much.

We lived in the next house for just under three years. The dark cloud in this case was, ostensibly, exorbitant property taxes on a huge house that didn't really suit us but was in fact due to an older boy two doors away who was a worse bully than I at that age.

From there we tried an old stucco house on a too-busy street and lasted less than a year. During that year we purchased a small fixer-upper down the street which I rehabbed and then managed as a rental for the next four years.

From the stucco place, we finally landed in a home where we stayed in bliss and love for fifteen years, until the boys were grown and gone; where we buried our cat, Mr. Kidders, in the corner of the back yard behind the pine trees we planted around the fire pit we created amidst pea gravel and homemade benches at the end of a flagstone path almost obscured by fragrant mother-of-thyme ground cover; where we often ate as a family beneath the shade of the wisteria vine on the deck I rebuilt; where the tire swing hung from the big locust tree until a storm blew it down; where the adjustable basketball hoop stood aside the driveway and I constantly tweaked the height to get the boys to jump higher for the alley-oops; where bedroom walls transformed from clouds and trains to baseball to snowboard posters and dream-catchers; where touchdowns were caught while diving onto the Lovesac in the basement; where tempers flared over the no cell phones upstairs policy; where a TV got thrown over the deck because two boys couldn't work it out; where Nana and Papa came for dinner once a week at least; where I perfected strawberry-rhubarb pie, Irish soda bread and crab risotto; where we rehabbed three-and-a-half bathrooms; where we mistakenly left the garage up overnight countless times and never got robbed; where music played every day; where torso-sized dents in basement drywall were repaired; where the tri-color beech amazed us every spring; where we played catch and Wiffle ball and I'd shout "This week in baseball!" when a great play was made; where we were safe; where we healed; where we laughed, cried, burped and passed gassers; where the boys went from sippy cups to wine glasses; where thousands of bedtime stories were read and told; where friends visited; where vacations to Keystone, Harbor Springs, the Y of the Rockies, The Black Hills, Costa Rica and the Great Wolf Lodge were launched; where a full length screenplay named "Ash" was written and produced; where "Jackie Wilson Said" and "Rocky Mountain High" played super loud on the living room stereo to alert sleepy boys upstairs that breakfast was being served in about three to four minutes.

And where I can only slowly drive by now and simultaneously feel in awe of the life I've had and agony over how out of reach it is to grasp. It's mostly awe, and with it joy. The agony is just knowing that I can't walk in the old garage, take a piece of sidewalk chalk in each hand, and create a street scene in the driveway for the trikes, scooters, skateboards, and bicycles of my boys' dreams.

My heart aches at times, thinking of how quickly the days of dadderhood passed, and I am so happy that I lived each day the way I did, present, grateful, whole. It helps tremendously that I didn't take any of it for granted, making a life with Katie and being a father to our boys. How miserable my life would be today if I had been otherwise disengaged or distracted and now wanting those days, any of them, back again.

I honestly don't want them back. I'm good. No regrets.

Here's the difference as I see it. When I was an athlete, it was essential that one be able to play with pain, and to do so meant that one had paid the price, done the work, been in the game, put forth the effort to be the best. Win or lose, the pain one felt during and after a hard practice or game was a badge of honor. On the other hand, when I was injured, I simply couldn't play. It meant I was broken for a time, and others would take my place.

So, when I write that I ache today, that it is sometimes painful to revisit the former days of dadderhood, it is a glorious pain I feel.

And I am still in the game! My spirit is not injured by regret. I'm not on the sidelines, or literally on the sidewalk outside our old home, fighting off nagging tears and spoken banes watching the ghosts of my boys playing and growing without me.

This is not to say that men who didn't, don't or can't spend as much quality time with their kids are any less a father. My own dad spent very little time with me, but he was a great dad, as I've tried to relate in these pages. And even though there were times when I was a boy that I wished he was around more, we both lived long enough for me to understand the role he played and for me to be able to tell him how thankful I was. Which brings me to something that I want both my sons to know.

Seamus and Graham, I want you both to know that I feel your love and gratitude for your mom and me and the life we share together. You left nothing unsaid, and for that you may rest with pain when we're gone, but not injury. We've had an amazing life, one that I hope continues for years and years to come. Just know that when the day comes that we pass away, you Seamus and you Graham, gave a thousand times more love and life than we ever imagined possible when Katie was pregnant with you.

And I wouldn't be completely forthright if I didn't share the following cautionary tale to any moms and dads that may read this someday.

To all of you unconditional lovers out there, specifically of children, but it probably holds for lovers of spouses and partners and friends, there is probably going to come a time, as it did for me, when those you love push back, want distance, appear ungrateful, don't want you around. This happened with both my sons, but I felt it more acutely with Seamus, probably because he was older and came to this place in his life first. It came on gradually but peaked in high school.

They were the darkest days of my dadderhood, because after being all-in, a stay-at-home dad, present from infancy nearly every day, it hurt like hell when I perceived that I wasn't needed or wanted. I took it personally for a time. I became depressed. I felt that in some ways my work was done. And in my worst moments I thought it wouldn't matter if I was gone.

The critical words there are, "I perceived." It took the wisdom of Katie and my friends and fellow dads, Dan deRegnier and Chris Paluch, to literally shed light on my darkness. They taught me that these were necessary steps a boy must take to become his own man. That I shouldn't take it personally. That the boys weren't pushing me away so much as finding themselves. That I just needed to be there for them because, after all I had given, all they really needed from me for a while was time.

Yes, Katie and Dan and Chris, you are beautiful to me.

And in one of those serendipitous Spotify-music-on-shuffle moments, as I read over what I've written today, Dan Fogelberg comes through again with "The Leader of the Band." He says at the end of that song that he doesn't think he told his dad "I love you" often enough.

Seamus and Graham, you said it a ton, and the thanks are there, they are ours to take from and give the universe whenever we ask.

19
Rita

In July 2022 I turned 61. It was my first birthday since learning the identity of my birth mother, Rita Perquin, the previous autumn, following a DNA connection made between two of her nephews and me on one of the ancestry websites. It turns out I have quite a few first cousins, along with an aunt, Rita's youngest sister. I have no known half-siblings, as I was Rita's only child and I know nothing of my biological father.

I spent a lot of time thinking of Rita on my birthday. I wish I could be writing of how I spent my day with her, sharing stories of our lives in the years after I left the hospital at five days of age. But Rita has been dead since July 10, 1987, just shy of my 26th birthday. While I was working as an actor in Chicago, she was living in Seattle, Washington.

The birth mother of my imagination is almost the antithesis of Rita. I always pictured her to be in her late-teens, single, too young to begin a family or be a single mother, who married later in life and had children that would one day be happy to be part of a beautiful reunion between their mom and me, their half-brother. In fact, Rita was 27 years old when I was born and had a career as a registered nurse. The only things Rita shared with my imagined heroine were being single and Catholic.

I was recently asked if I would rather live in ignorance with the romantic image of what my birth mother might be or with the painful reality of what I've come to learn. Without a second's hesitation, I would choose the latter.

Rita is one of the primary motivating forces in writing this memoir. So often in the writing, I imagine Rita, now eighty-eight years old, reading the story of the boy she gave life to so long ago. In so many ways, this is my ode to Rita, my song of gratitude, my love letter to adoption and my testimonial to love. Where would I be without any of it?

My adoption file is inaccessible to me, locked away at the Catholic Charities office in Des Moines. However, a very compassionate adoption caseworker, Tiffany, offered to search my records after I reached out to her and explained my circumstances, basically that I already knew who my birth mother was and there was little left for her to protect or hide. I wanted to learn whatever I could about Rita and any details surrounding my adoption.

It was because of Tiffany's kindness and efforts that I learned the address of the apartment where Rita lived with her friend, Mary, for the final four months of her pregnancy while working as a nurse at the hospital where I was born. That building still stands and I've spent longing minutes parked outside imagining my birth mother walking in and out the main door, walking the neighborhood, probably walking to and from work through the pedestrian-friendly streets on nice days.

Tiffany gave me the name of the building where I lived for the first two weeks of my life, up until I was placed with my mom and dad. That institution was called Christ Child Home, and the mansion, now a law office, still stands on Grand Avenue. I drive past it frequently, and although I know the lawyer whose name fronts the bill rather well (his son played baseball with my sons), I have yet to take up his attorney wife's offer to tour the home where a plaque hangs honoring the home's history as a Catholic orphanage.

But the pearl of my adoption file is the handwritten letter Rita wrote to a local priest in my hometown on the advice of her parish priest in Philadelphia about a month before she moved. Tiffany made a copy and sent it to me.

The letter, seven pages in length, is written with beautiful cursive penmanship. She introduces herself, twenty-six at the time, an immigrant to Montreal from Holland at the age of eighteen where she studied nursing at St. Mary's Hospital School of Nursing. How she moved with her family to Washington, D.C., when her father took a teaching job at Catholic University of America. She talks of her failed attempts to reach my biological father whose name is mysteriously left out of the missive and I find myself caring less and less who he is and why Rita couldn't reach him.

In a telling passage, Rita talks about the potential nursing job.

"I don't want to cause any kind of embarrassment, especially not to Mary or her sister. When Father Reilly told me you would be able to get a job for me at Mercy for a little while, I only thought of what that would mean to me. Apart from the financial advantage, it would also mean less time I have to spend doing very little, and I'm afraid of what boredom could do to me. But no matter how much I would like a job, any kind for that matter, I have to think of the consequences to others. Therefore, I hope you understand me when I say that I cannot work at Mercy Hospital."

There must have been, in 1961, an enormous stigma to a mature Catholic woman having a baby out of wedlock, let alone a teenager, and I think it says a lot about Rita that she was more concerned about preventing a disgrace to her friend and her family than having a much-desired job at Mercy Hospital. And since she did take that job, I choose to believe her friend, Mary, convinced her that there would be no harm. I wonder if Mary is still alive. I sure would love to find out, to thank her for being a friend to Rita, but Tiffany blackened out her maiden name in the letter for ethical reasons and no amount of pleading from me would change her mind.

(As a side note, I did my own investigating and learned the identity of Rita's nursing friend from clues Rita wrote in the letter. I hoped to be able to reach out to her, to ask what she recalls of those months they lived together. Sadly, she has died.)

Just before closing out the letter, Rita wrote:

"It's so difficult to make definite plans when I don't really know what to do, except pray that my parents, sisters, and brother never find out why I'm really going away… Whatever sacrifices I have to make, I'll make. It will be worth it."

It's left to me to grapple with the reality that a Catholic Church which preached love, forgiveness and acceptance only to thrust such shame and guilt upon unwed mothers, a church that I've turned my back upon along with all organized religion, set in motion and enabled events that led to my birth and beautiful placement with my mom and dad and provided my life a spiritual home for so many years in my youth and young adulthood. I've rightly and happily chosen to be grateful, not cynical, toward the Catholic Church for providing a safe and nurturing environment for Rita to give birth and place her baby in a loving home, without the poison of wry suspicions of an institution merely interested in securing their numbers.

I wouldn't be writing this memoir had Rita chosen to keep me and raise me. It is impossible to conjure up where I'd be or whether I'd even be alive. However, I think it's quite possible Rita would be alive today if she had given the middle finger to her faith and the societal norms surrounding her, come clean to her family, and figured out a way to raise me while pursuing her career. Her life's course would have drastically altered, and it must be nigh on impossible that she would have ended up with the man that took her life and then his own on July 10, 1987 (eight years to the day prior to my dad's fatal heart attack). Rita was 53 years old.

Her abusive husband had lost his job and his troubles with alcohol worsened. After a violent altercation, Rita had him arrested but relented when it came time to press charges. Two weeks later, while Rita was reading in bed, wearing a t-shirt that said, "Club Bed," the bastard shot her two times in the chest. She died instantly. He then called his brother in Tacoma, confessed what he had done, hung up the phone and shot himself in the head. Detectives at the scene found Rita's address book and phoned her family back east. I did the math, Rita let her husband out of jail on their anniversary.

It was heartbreaking when Rita's sister, Johanna, told me this story. Oh Rita. If you'd have had my love in your life, you wouldn't have needed the companionship of a desperate man. That's not to say that a son's love is all a woman needs, but when love exists in a life it becomes harder for its imposter to gain entry.

And so, I am a freaking flippin' Olympian when it comes to mental gymnastics. I have won all-around gold and scored tens on every apparatus of hypothetical what-if, why-not and how-could. None of it matters in the end. The fact is, Rita is in me and I'm right here. At this moment she is alive, all eighty-eight years alive. I am sitting beside her, holding her hand. In a minute or two or twenty of simply savoring the image of being together, the first thing I will say is, "Thanks for having me."

20
Soap Box Soliloquy

Abortion was not legal when I was born. Rita had little choice but to give birth to her unwanted child. That's the truth. Being a devout Catholic, she may still have chosen to give birth if abortion had been an option in 1961; I'll never know. What I know from the letter she wrote to the priest is that, in the early months of her pregnancy, she didn't want her family to know she was pregnant; from that I could conclude that she'd have had an abortion. From that same letter, Rita stated she was determined and committed to taking great care while she carried me to term; from that, and her devout Catholicism, I must believe she'd have given birth to me regardless.

I can understand why abortion is a religious issue, but it needn't be one in my opinion. It is a women's issue. If a person is religious and believes in heaven and hell and God and judgment, then why can't they let women choose and leave it to their God to be the judge?

I know, pro-life people say they need to be the voice and fight for the God-given rights of the unborn that have no voice. In principle, it's a noble thought, a beautiful feeling. It's a feeling I share. But it's not my decision to make! And I'm in no position to judge anyone who makes it. If I were religious, I'd have to ask myself, if my god created the pregnant woman and gave her free will, what right do I have to intervene in that design? It seems audacious, arrogant, and vain.

Personally, I despise abortion. I despise the word. I want to call it "Feminapassio" or "Materpassio," compassion for the woman or mother. My heart aches for the women who must make that decision, often alone, and have to endure that painful procedure. I wish we lived in a world where abortion didn't exist, and there was another term for a procedure that terminated a pregnancy that threatened the life of the woman. Feminapassio. I wish we lived in a world where men and women revered the act of intercourse as the most consequential form of creation and not a base form of conquest. We don't live in that world, never have, probably never will. Until we do, women should have the right to choose. It really is that simple. In my mind, it's Pro-Choice, not Pro-Abortion.

To my knowledge, I've only been a part of three pregnancies, all with Katie: our miscarriage and our two sons. But if I'm being honest, I don't really know if I've been responsible for a woman needing an abortion. Although no woman ever came to me to say I was the father to a fetus she was carrying, if that had happened, I could say without a shred of piety or self-praise that I would have supported her choice. I would have been a father if she'd have allowed me. I was that fetus once, how could I do otherwise? Alternatively, painful as it would be for both of us, I would have regrettably let it go if she chose an abortion. I was that fetus once, how could I feel otherwise?

Those are my thoughts, shared only because I am the result of an unplanned and unwanted pregnancy and a planned and very much desired adoption.

21
For The Boys

I'd like to address one of the reasons I am writing this memoir. I want my sons to know me better. And if they ever have children, perhaps this story will reach them as well. Someday, all that will be left of me is these pages, a few semi-durable goods, and the memories that live in the hearts of those who survive me. That is all the immortality I need. When I die, I wish to be cremated and hope my ashes will be strewn or buried uncontained in a place my sons want to visit, perhaps a grove of redwoods near mountains for Seamus and the ocean for Graham (as opposed to a cemetery plot in a town they may not need to see again).

I want my boys to know that raising them with their mother truly was the greatest joy of my lifetime.

I could fill a hundred more pages with the most mundane precious details of the part of my life I lived in that "Dadderhood of My Sweetest Dreams." Judging by how many pages are left in this book, it's clear that most of them will live on only in the hearts and inner rings of a few. Anyway, how can I describe how it felt to hear Nanci Griffith's The Dustbowl Symphony version of "The Wing and the Wheel" for the first time while waiting in the car line at a preschool with tears streaming down my face, and how hearing it now for the odd hundredth time tightens my chest and floods my eyes remembering how we wouldn't even get out of the parking lot but go over to the swings and play for sweet moments with Hammy and Anne, nowhere we had to be and nowhere else I wanted to be. And now I listen to Kenny Chesney's "There Goes My Life" and weep again like the first time I heard it because I live my life with my heart split open for the givers and takers I choose. How did I know then that both my boys would end up out west living their best versions of themselves and what more could a father want?

I'm deep into my autumn years and my boys are nearing the end of their spring. There's not much left for me to tend to in their garden, but they know their mom and I are standing at the porch listening, willing to pull the odd weed when asked or provide some shelter from a storm. I'm grateful that it's a garden we love to see and get to touch from time to time. I take such comfort knowing that the soil their mom and I nurtured will sustain them for as long as they live. And when we talk on the phone, when they visit us or we them, when I listen to the songs we loved, when I drive by a Little League ballfield, when I make pancakes, when I see kids playing basketball in a driveway, see a parent and child holding hands across a parking lot, see a kid in a shopping cart, see a car with flame decals… the countless images alive in my mind. Do you see where I'm going with this? The here and now and the eternity that my heart holds is all the divinity I need.

There was a time in my life when I had a sense of my destiny but had hard doubts I would meet it. It was when I lived in Ireland with Ted, and I heard a different Nanci Griffith song for the first time, "Late Night Grande Hotel." I wept for other reasons when I heard lines like "All my life I've left my troubles by the door. Leavin' is all I've ever known before." Shortly after that,

I met Kassandra and went down that road for a spell thinking I'd found it. It took me a while to finally find that place where I wouldn't want to leave, in Katie's arms and in my two sons' lives. That is my heaven, where I will remain until there is not a soul left to remember me.

I think it's a Native American belief that a person lives on as long as they are remembered. As an actor, that's one of my jobs. It also prevents me from taking anything for granted. That is why, prior to every performance, I say aloud the names of every person that has passed that I've acted with or who inspired me or nurtured me along my path as an actor: Freda Nahas, Ray McHenry, "Doc" Coleman, Jim Mitchell, Trudy Kelly, Catherine Price, John Sterchi, John Mohrlein, P.J. Brown, Rick Sandoval, and mom and dad. I bring those past loves, who no longer play, on stage to play with me.

My sons have already lost friends in their young lives, to cancer, to suicide. The grief left in the wake of those young lives is imaginable to me, and I don't know if I could survive it. I hope I never find out. It is the only thing in the world that I fear.

The truth is that my life is an exhilaratingly beautiful, loving, grateful, desperate dance between the bliss of being in a world with Katie, Seamus, Graham and a handful of friends, and the terror of living in a world that doesn't care. But that is life, the terrifying beauty of life. The trick to thriving in it seems to lie in the ability to choose beauty, to drown oneself in it and tell the fear as often as needed to go fuck itself. To never let the fear stand in the way of love.

My mom and dad ached to have a love like that and they adopted me. How lucky was that? How lucky was I? Here I sit, a 61-year-old man crying like a baby thinking of my life as an adoptee. It's almost unfathomable to me how I ended up here, yet here I am.

I also weep for my birth mother, Rita, who gave me life and lost hers before I could find her. She did all she could do for me, and her wildest dreams for me came true. They really did. But I wish I could take a pill that would let me remember my moments with her before I left her for our eternity. I was probably crying then, too. Maybe she was as well, and that's why I'm so emotional. Maybe that's why it feels like my chest is caving in every time I say goodbye to someone I love. Every time. But I wouldn't have it any other way.

From time to time over the years, I've had to ponder, to varying degrees, the idea that I was given away. I reckon it's a thought that many infant adoptees must reconcile, regardless of the circumstances of their placement, be it in a home of love or one of neglect. The thought arrives and must be handled.

All those years I pined to learn about Rita, to someday find her, turns out she was with me all along. It has taken me a long time to learn that. Shawn Colvin asks, in her cover of "This Must Be the Place," if someone will love her until her heart stops. Rita, I know you will.

22
I'm Wired That Way

I have a photo of Rita that I obtained in a text from the son of Johanna, Rita's younger sister. The picture is of her as a little girl in Zeist, The Netherlands, maybe six years old, wearing what is probably her father's fedora, smiling while looking at something to the right of the photographer. If someone cropped her older sister from the photo and stuck it in the photo album my mom made for me when I turned 18, I would think it was me.

There's no question Rita was my mother. She was long-limbed and lean like me, and I even see traces of her face in my boys. Obviously, all my physical attributes and athleticism came from Rita and the mystery man. I have them to thank for my innate ability to run full speed toward where a ball is heading and place my hand at a point where I can catch it before it hits the ground. I could do this in the sandlots of my childhood, the prime of my collegiate days, and when playing in the Mid-Iowa Baseball League in my fifties.

I played in that league for about nine years, until my age 59 season. In many ways, it made up for the baseball life I might have lived in my late teens and early twenties. I played on a 25+ and 35+ team the first couple seasons, went 35+ and 45+ for a few more, and ended my "career" playing 40+ and 48+. Man was it fun! Usually two games a week, from June until October. The dudes I was playing with and against had pretty much all played high school ball and many played in college. All were kids at heart, even if some of them were jerks who argued with umpires, threw their bats, or just had pine tar up their ass.

I modeled my game after Ted Williams; all comparisons ended with the fact neither of us wore batting gloves. Nine times out of ten I slid headfirst, as the hole in the elbow of the compression shirt I wore under my uniform and have on right now will affirm. In my age 58 season I hit a home run over the 310' fence in left center and ran the bases like I'd done it fifty times even though I wanted to do cartwheels and somersaults like my son Graham would do after scoring a goal in youth soccer. I played outfield mostly, but over the seasons played every position save pitcher and catcher. I didn't have the knees to play catcher and the teams I played on had plenty of pitching depth. In my final game, I made the catch of my life. The baseball gods gave me a gift I'll always cherish when I think about my life as an athlete.

It happened while playing in the championship game with the 40+ Grays. I was playing right field. The batter was right-handed, so I played in a little to defend against a potential weak hit to the opposite field. Sure enough, the ball came my way, a sinking liner tailing away from me toward the first base line. At full speed I ran in, laid myself out, airborne, headfirst, and caught the ball about three inches above the ground, about twenty feet beyond the infield dirt. When I looked up, the pitcher, Jason Henry, was standing on the mound pointing at me and slapping the side of his glove. Then, to my shock because I considered him a friend and excellent teammate, the center fielder, Aaron Quinn, said, "If you'd have been playing in more, you wouldn't have had to dive like that."

I didn't even acknowledge the comment, but it stung. Clearly, I'm over it, can't you tell? But it was a bullshit thing to say about a catch I had never seen anyone at any age make in all my years in the league and would have made ESPN's Top Ten if a major leaguer had done it. I was fifty-fucking-eight years old. It's how I played the game. The only way I could play it.

And I'm so grateful the baseball gods gave me that ball to run down, because the highlight reel in my mind needed something nice to end on. You see, I stopped playing in the 30+ league a couple years prior when it became apparent I was too old for those young bucks. In one of the last games I played in that league, I balked at a catchable long fly ball to left field because I didn't want to run into the fence, and later that game, completely misplayed and overran a high fly ball to shallow left-center after calling off the shortstop and center fielder; it landed about five feet to my right. DOH!

It was a great time. My boys got to see me play. Katie came to games. My old theater professor, "Doc" Coleman, a huge baseball fan and season ticket holder with the Iowa Cubs, came to see me play a couple times before he died.

In the end, I quit playing, because when my knees told me I couldn't go 100% and throw my body around like I was a crash-test dummy, I knew it wouldn't be fun anymore. I'm not "pinch-runner guy." I sat out my age 60 season because it hurt to walk. I had my knees replaced before my age 61 season. And because I want these new "wheels" to carry me to the finish line, I'll call it good. I'll miss playing baseball. I already miss the way the thought of playing carried me through the Midwestern winters and provided motivation to get my ass in the gym. But worse is the idea of playing this summer, catching whatever balls I can get to, perhaps playing first base because I'm not mobile enough to play anywhere else, running at less than top speed, never stealing a base, unable to score from first base on a ball hit to the gap.

And please understand that I'm not dissing "pinch-runner guy;" he's just the player that wants to bat but, for reasons of his own, doesn't want to run the bases. (Sometimes a player might be nursing a pulled hamstring or ankle strain and chooses to hit but declares a pinch runner if he gets on base; he's not "pinch-runner guy," he's just working back from an injury.) "Pinch-runner guy" is slow, typically overweight, doesn't want to strain himself, basically feels that he puts his team at a disadvantage if he's on the basepaths and many times doesn't even play in the field. But I do respect and admire "pinch-runner guy" because he loves the game, loves the camaraderie of the dugout, loves being a teammate, and wants to contribute in any way he can. The beautiful thing about the Mid-Iowa Baseball League is that there is a welcome home for everyone, the former low-level pro player, former college player, athlete, and kid at heart. I'd be welcome on three teams I've played with if I was willing to play at probably 75 or 80 percent of my ability. I'm just not wired that way and I'd rather be home with Katie.

How am I wired? Does DNA reach into my brainscape more than I would, for lack of a better word, think? I've seen where there have been studies into musical ability that suggest it is hereditary, not that I'm musical much beyond an ability to strum a few chords, pick a little, and appreciate most any genre. There are studies that suggest behaviors like depression and empathy are expressions written into one's genome. It has me thinking of nature vs. nurture.

Being adopted, most ruminations into what made me the way I am, beyond the obvious, are parlor games at best. I don't spend a lot of time mulling them over. The fact that Rita worked in nursing and health care for the entirety of her adult life tells me that she must have had an abundance of nurturing and empathy in her being. Combine that with the selfless love I was raised with, then I suppose it's the reason staying home with my children felt as natural and uncomplicated as anything I've ever taken on and it never felt like a sacrifice to some other calling. And that, dear reader, is as close as I can come in this most unscientific study to saying that caring and nurturing is hereditary and environmental, and I'd like to think Rita is as much a part of how I loved as why I lived.

23
You're Not My Teacher

From the years 2007 to 2011, I was immersed in writing, producing, directing, and acting in a feature film I called "Ash." After taking it to some film festivals in 2010-11, I decided I needed something else to do to fill my days while the boys were in school. Thus, I finally used my education degree in the autumn of 2012 after I updated my credentials and obtained a substitute teaching certificate. Initially, I offered my services to elementary and high schools. After a year of bouncing around, I ditched elementary schools and public high schools and worked solely at my old Catholic high school, now called Dowling Catholic, mostly because they kept me busy and it was easier than saying no every morning to everyone else.

I have tremendous respect for second-grade teachers. I experienced the most grueling, tiresome, patience-straining month of subbing one day in a second-grade class. Seriously, there was more drama in that one day at Christ the King than you'd find backstage at a kid's weekend dance competition.

It started innocently enough when I was greeted at the door of the classroom with a hug by a darling little girl. I don't think I had my coat off before I was hugged two more times, and I was searching my clothing for Webkinz labels by the time the bell rang to start the day.

I must have missed the lecture in Elementary Ed. that taught to never trust a child that hugs you more than three times before the day begins.

Within fifteen minutes she urgently told me for the first of many times, "That's not how our teacher does it!" My use of an exclamation mark in the quote would have a tear dripping from it if my keyboard spoke seven-year-old. Later that morning she drove the boy next to her to such lengths of frustration that he dug his fingernails into the flesh of her forearm just short of the required depth to produce blood but deep enough to leave tiny crescent moons in her skin for the remainder of the day; her arm looked like the flag of an Arab nation. I didn't know this was happening until I heard her shriek and wail. I did my best to bring the situation under control with genuine care and compassion but did manage to cast an aside to the youngster that I knew how he felt…just kidding. I was appalled that the parents of that boy let the nails grow so long and that the teacher didn't have nail clippers in her desk. I separated the kids, which caused a whole new set of problems because, you guessed it, "That's not where our teacher seats us!" Every time I assembled the kids to go somewhere, lunch, recess, music, P.E., there was a conflagration over whose turn it was to be first in the line. Story time finally, mercifully arrived at the end of the day and was the highlight. I made the session extra-long and thank Christ the King none of the kids could tell time or I'd have certainly heard, "It's too early to start reading to us!!!" I love reading to kids, where I can make use of my particular set of skills in voice work and acting. We had a ball. At the end I couldn't help but ask if that was how their teacher did it, and one of the kids said, "No, she just reads to us."

I never took an assignment from that school again. They called me one day and I told them that I would, but that I suddenly decided to volunteer as a test patient at the local School for Blindfolded Nineteenth Century Dentistry Technique. But seriously, I no longer worked in any grade below fifth after that, for the rest of that first year.

The greatest experience I had in all my substitute teaching life came to me that year when I took a month-long assignment in fifth grade at St. Augustin Catholic School. Nancy Dowdle and Pat Hogan are two beautiful administrators and educators who led a school where respect and courtesy reigned, and the kids in that classroom were, every one of them, as kind to me as they were to each other. I'd never seen anything like it. I was elevated to tears on more than one occasion. Many wrote me beautiful letters on my last day in their classroom. I find myself getting choked up now thinking of them, and a little in awe at how different it was from my fifth-grade experience.

I also took a few gigs at my old grade school, St. Theresa's, that first year. I visited a lot of ghosts. A lot of ghosts, including a peek inside the old janitor's closet.

As I mentioned, I worked exclusively at my old high school from the fall of 2013 to the spring of 2018. Not many ghosts there because they almost completely renovated the place in my absence. But the auditorium and stage are still there, so I was frequently able to sneak in and pay my respects to my old drama teacher, Freda Nahas, when I subbed up in the arts area. The large round wooden tables that in my days served the 11-12 grade study hall now did their duty in one of the faculty areas. I could almost make out where Pete Porto and I wrote in eraser on the varnished surface of one table every word of the Eagles song "Desperado" our senior year, 1979.

I was amazed that there were three faculty members on staff that taught when I went to school and two of them remembered me, only because they were coaches (the other taught art).

It was always interesting to observe how full-time teachers treated me when I worked among them as a substitute. You know that adage about how you can tell a lot about someone by how they treat those who can't do anything for them? Every English teacher was cool, except for this one dude who you just wanted to tie to a chair and force him to watch Ricky Gervais YouTube videos all day. The male math teachers and the two engineering teachers were cool, but the female math teachers were a fairly haughty bunch. Hell, everyone knew I couldn't do much more than take attendance, distribute worksheets, and run the AV controls in any math class, but really, ladies? Today, from the lofty heights of hindsight, I can cut the math ladies some slack because they must have endured an unfair amount of condescension and mansplaining as they progressed in a predominantly male discipline. The majority of social studies teachers were coaches, much like when I was a student, so we got along very well. The science department was an odd mix of personalities, best summed up by the state of their respective desks; the most condescending teacher had an impeccable and spare desktop, and it took every atom of my anatomy not to mess with his area, rearrange the stapler with the AV remote, juxtapose the inbox and outbox trays, switch the caps on the varicolored dry erase markers, etc. The messy and disorganized earth science teacher left me no room to put my stuff and her classes reflected her lack of discipline. And even though I'd done well in college chemistry, biology, kinesiology, and astronomy classes, I quickly learned that it was best to play down to their expectations. The best thing about subbing in the foreign language department was studying the maps of foreign countries on the walls after I took attendance and got the students going on their work. I would drink margaritas with the Spanish teachers and strong beer with the German teacher, while the others left me dry.

It's no surprise that art and P.E. departments were where I felt most at home and where I was most welcomed. It got to the point where I was the person the school called whenever the P.E. department had a need; I could teach a yoga class, I knew my way around a weight room and when the athletes respect you then the rest fall in line.

The best thing to come out of my time substitute teaching was my friendship with Tim O'Neill. It's one I have to this day and one I hope to have as long as I live. Early on, after exchanging pleasantries and histories, he asked me if I ever painted. I said, "Yes." Next thing I knew we were painting an entire two-story exterior in two days and the rest, as they say, is history. I painted a lot of houses with Tim and his twin brother, Tom. We listened to good music, didn't take breaks, ate our lunches in about 15 minutes, and painted most houses in one day. I quit painting houses at the same time I stopped playing baseball; again, my knees said, "No more."

Substitute teaching at the high school I once attended was fairly easy work. I felt at home among the teachers, administrators and students and was made to feel welcome (until I wasn't, which I'll get to momentarily). The principal was very appreciative of the subs who worked in his building and never hesitated to say so when he crossed my path. There always seemed to be a few students who would thank me as they walked out after a class. With very few exceptions, I was always made to feel like a favored guest when I was working.

But part of me felt like a fraud because I was working in a Catholic school. I never let on to anyone that I wasn't religious and no longer believed in God. I suppose I should credit my years as a practicing Catholic and my acting chops for being able to dwell among them without being cast out to the netherlands of public schools.

First and foremost, I was a guest in their house. It would have been the epitome of classlessness and disrespect to not honor the beliefs of the students I was entrusted to teach. Subbing in the religion department was not a problem; I spoke the language, verbal and non-verbal alike.

I'm reminded of an experience I had while rehearsing for a production of "King Lear." One of the actors in my company (who has since been kicked to the curb), a self-proclaimed devout Christian, was questioning and mocking a guest artist in her teens who was wearing a cross necklace and had mentioned that she was Catholic. When I realized what he was doing, I pulled him aside and gave him a verbal throat punching for being such an arrogant bully and miserable human being. I then went to the young woman and apologized on behalf of the theater company. One wonders what kind of faith journey relishes in the abuse of another based on their beliefs.

My own faith journey has led me toward an embrace of reason and away from blind faith and God.

The first cracks in the foundation began in my late teens when I doubted the existence of places like Limbo and Purgatory, the principle of being born with Original Sin when we were allegedly born in the image and likeness of God, and my resentment of the pre-Eucharist prayer that said, "Lord, I am NOT WORTHY to receive you, but only say the word and I shall be healed." Even at an early age, I despised the way that prayer diminished me when, in fact, I felt worthy…except when I masturbated. For years, when I attended mass and the time came to pronounce that prayer, I just left out the word "not."

More cracks developed when I learned about the Catholic Church's sale of indulgences, read books like "The Power of Myth" and histories that included the conversions of native peoples; I've always felt akin to native peoples in history and seldom sympathized with the conqueror, probably because I was raised Irish and, according to my DNA, am half Celt.

It took a long, long time to unravel and untrench years of teaching and believing. It's not like being a kid and figuring out there isn't a Santa Claus. And then there's that whole comfort level in believing in everything that believing promises, like a place to go when we and our loved ones die, for example. I just don't believe any of it.

Very few people know this about me because I think faith, or the absence of it, is very personal. I just don't think anyone really needs to know unless they're like that prick in my theater company a few years ago and tries to shove theirs in my face. Since I don't really have any of those people in my life, it rarely comes up.

It does come up in social media circles quite a bit and I usually unfriend the folks who are most adamant. I don't argue, it's their room or feed, I just leave.

I recently left for good, quietly, the virtual room of a woman, the wife of a college teammate, who insisted that prayer helped save the life of Buffalo Bills player Damar Hamlin. She couldn't accept that it was solely the work of first responders on the football field and medical personnel at the Cincinnati hospital.

It follows that if one doesn't believe in God, one doesn't believe in most prayers. But even if I believed in God, I'd have serious doubts about prayer. Take the case of my younger son's friend that died of cancer at the age of 15. Tens of thousands of prayers were offered up to God to spare him and intervene in his healing. When those prayers go unanswered, the typical response is, "God called him home," or "It is God's plan, and we can't presume to understand God," or words along that line. Also, when a 65-year-old person who has done harm with their life survives the same diagnosis after undergoing the same treatments and few prayers, it is again God's will and prayer that tipped the scales and saved the ill person…and thank God for the excellent medical team! It doesn't matter that I don't understand how or why a God might choose who lives or dies, but what kind of Creator would take the 15-year-old and spare the 65-year-old? And if we can never know God's plan, and God will do whatever she intends, what good is prayer? It seems to me that prayer is something people do to ease their feeling of helplessness in the face of crisis. Is there really a God up there who is thinking, "Dang, if I'd have just received 512 more prayers, I'd have spared little Martha, and her family all that grief"?

I prefer to let people know that I love them and if they are ailing that I hope for them the strength to realize their most desired outcome.

As far as prayers of gratitude go, I can feel thankful, and express my gratitude to others, without needing to include God.

My boys might read this and say, "But dad, you are always praying to our guardian angels and thanking them when we make it where we're going." To which I will respond that prayer can be a non-religious act. Please let me explain.

When I pray to our guardian angels, I am being lazy and using the language of religion to simply conjure up the combined wisdom, experience, instinct/intuition, and care needed to navigate the indifference of a world. It is a petition or a thank you to the spirit of all that I have been and all that made me and all that I have tried to instill in you, to guard and guide you in ways that will hopefully keep you safe. If we want to truly live in the world, then we are helpless when it comes to the randomness and frailty of life. But I will never stop reminding you, planting the seeds of wisdom and respect for life and love that have sustained me to this day; that's all the prayer I have. I hope it will sustain you for decades after I'm gone; that's all the heaven I need. Boys, when I tell you that Grampa Tom and Grandma Moira are two of your guardian angels, all I mean is that I believe the things they instilled in me live on in you.

I don't need God to love my neighbor, to be grateful, to be faithful or be a believer, to see beauty in the world, to recognize the sublime, to feel ecstasy. I don't want churches, synagogues and mosques destroyed. I don't need a devil to explain evil. I won't judge those who do.

We are all on this journey together. One hope I have is that we'll come to a place as human beings where one day we respect each other regardless of what we do or don't believe. But honestly, wouldn't it be nice to have an opportunity to work through our human frailties without the added baggage of religion and rejoice in our victories for our own sake? I, for one, think we'd be better off.

If I had a prayer for humanity, it would be this: Let us all treat this planet and each other as if this is all we have and all that our future generations will ever have. If you believe in God and heaven, err on the side of caution, just in case you're wrong, and treat the miracle of our creation as if it is the only heaven your God intended.

I don't care for the term "atheist" because there's too much negative baggage. If it mattered to me, I'd coin a term for a person who doesn't believe in God, has no interest in arguing with those who do, no interest in proselytizing a non-belief and who really, really likes gospel music. I love the singing that such passion and belief inspires. I love the choir and the blending surge of voices, the harmonies. Of all the art forms that religion has inspired over the ages, I think gospel music may be the purest. All the breathtakingly beautiful painting and sculpture and architecture and poetry could conceivably have been realized in other manifestations by the artists without religion. But would we have gospel music without Christianity? I wonder. On that note, I am cueing up The Brooklyn Tabernacle Choir's recording of "Midnight Cry" on my Bluetooth speaker while dinner cooks in the oven. It's almost enough to make me believe again.

In the early spring of 2018, the drama teacher at Dowling Catholic announced that he was leaving to take an assistant principal job at a local grade school. I applied for the job, was a finalist, but was ultimately passed over for the other candidate (who lasted one year in the job). Shortly after the decision was made, the president and principal invited me to a follow-up meeting. They explained that I was a fantastic candidate but it came down to the fact that I lacked two credits for the English teaching endorsement on my license (the departing teacher taught an English and a journalism class in addition to his drama classes). Even though I outlined in detail during the final interview exactly how I planned to obtain the credits sooner than the required time allowed by the State of Iowa, they responded that, being an elite private school, they made it a policy to not hire teachers who didn't have all the necessary endorsements for the position being filled. They pointed out that many rural schools need to make those exceptions, but they had the luxury of not needing to do that.

I never worked there again.

In the end, I was okay with their decision and in many ways grateful, but in the moment, it hurt like the hell I imagined when I was a kid. I would have been amazing in that job, maybe too amazing for the likes of the man who was the head of the drama and debate department whom I frequently subbed for and who sat in on all the interviews.

Finally, of all the jobs I've applied for and not been hired, for all the acting gigs I've auditioned for and not been cast, there is only one rejection that still stings me to this day, almost seven years later. I auditioned for the role of Willy Loman in the Iowa Stage Theater

Company production of "Death of a Salesman" in 2016. When I learned I wasn't cast, I felt as gutted as all the fish I knifed in Alaska. My dad was a traveling salesman, like Willy. It's the one role I believe I was born to perform and have dreamed of playing since I first read the play in college. And to make matters worse, the director cast the same guy I had verbally throat punched for chastising that girl a few weeks prior to the audition. Yeah, that guy. It's important that I'm not the only one to say this: he sucked. As I said, the rejection left a mark. I almost quit acting afterwards, and I am now very selective about what plays and people get my time.

24

So, You Think You're An Artist?

The Artist is one who has been gifted by their genetics to access that which is most sublime and terrifying about being human and, either by courage or the crucible of their surroundings or the patronage of a benefactor, has the grit and stamina to paint, sculpt, write, compose, and exhibit the very world they expose, elevate, and enlighten.

Sometimes, the work transcends time and borders, and reaches generations. To me, the Artists are the most amazing and awe-inspiring individuals in every era of human history. I don't measure this by the impact of this discovery or that invention because these things are usually very collaborative and merely attributed to an individual. I certainly don't measure this by one's material possessions or any accumulation of wealth. Generals and politicians don't impress me. And from the last chapter it's clear I don't believe that anyone who proclaims their life or teaching or prophecy to be a provenance from something supernatural like God or astrology belongs on any kind of pedestal, regardless of how many people they inspire or institutions they've sired.

(There is a coffee shop in my head where I am currently sitting with a few friends talking about art, church patronage, God, and whether Artists like Michelangelo could have done the work they did in a secular world.)

I don't consider myself an Artist. To me, acting is a craft. Actors don't become Artists simply because not everyone can do it well, or because it requires some technique and practice, or because it's taught in the fine arts department of a school. I think few actors ascend to that level of devotion required of a true Artist. So, when I'm around actors who proclaim that lofty title as their own, I swallow my words like I do around the religious. If someone thinks of themselves as an Artist, who am I to argue?

I'm probably pissing off a lot of actors here, and I'll throw dancers into the mix while I'm at it. Dancers are very graceful athletes who use their bodies in beautiful ways to represent the ideas of the composer and choreographer, much in the way that actors use words (and to a lesser extent their bodies) to represent the words of the writer.

At his trial, he was asked if he'd concede to being an Artist with a small "a." He refused. He simply said, "If you need to label me, call me a Creative."

And so it was that a jury of his peers found him guilty of heresy and condemned him to either watching reruns of the secretly taped opening night production of Iowa Stage's "Death of A Salesman" for one week, or living in exile in a sod cabin in western Nebraska for the remainder of his days. On days when the wind is right, he can be heard as far away as Valentine, quoting Shakespeare to the crickets and cranes.

25

Where the Trees Dance

Who are the MVPs of your life? I'm asking this because my mind is drifting between how I wrap up this memoir and the view outside my window. The ground outside is covered in snow but the scurry of squirrels is undaunted as they cavort about the trunks and branches of the four tall pines and ornamental trees; the pine boughs that didn't survive the recent storm lie on the ground like unstrung guitars on the floor of a luthier's shop. The squirrels don't seem bothered by their diminished playground the way I was when my mom and dad's next-door neighbor put up a fence in their backyard. And even though I'd much rather see the branches up high than burn their logs next winter, I'll be grateful for the warmth, and listen to their sap pop like it's summer talking.

It has me thinking about Earth's MVP. Was there ever a time it was humanity? Yeah, I didn't think so either. I'm going to fill up an immodest glass of red wine, channel Mother Earth, and come up with as many realistic candidates as I can before I drain it.

"Earth, tell me, what is your MVP for all time? Erosion? Plate tectonics? The tilt of your axis? Ice? Wind? The sun? The lifecycle? The Amazon River Basin? Sequoia and redwood trees (co-MVPs)? Fire? Peat bogs in Ireland? Lilacs? Crickets? Victoria Falls? Dinosaurs? Golden retrievers? Golf course architects? Red Rocks Amphitheater? Elysian Fields? Grapevines?"

Once the wine started talking, I refilled my glass, sat back in my chair, and waited for the Earth's reply.

To which, one refill later, I heard the following:

"Trees are invariably my MVP. They are the most glorious expression of all that I hide and all that the sun and rain provide. They offer shelter from the storm and a message for your forlorn. They bend to Connemara wind and are a place for birds to live in. On a stone cliffside they'll thrive, in the desert they'll survive, and their roots keep the hillside alive. They are at once fellable and infallible, a wistful gift for your mill insatiable. With a history stored in rings, their branches help me see horizons and hear things. They dwell in sediment, weep, fruit, leave, pine, cleave, bark, burn, smoke, and turn. Father to my mother, sister to my brother, testament to possibility and bell tower to thee."

I looked long and hard at my empty wine glass and considered what I'd just heard. My playfully smug reflection peered back at me. In that moment of silence, sensing it was my turn to talk, I said to my glass, "Hey, I think I'll wait until tomorrow morning. It's weird, you staring at me like that, and coffee doesn't judge."

"Suit yourself," came the wry reply. "When you're ready to rhyme there's more wine on the shelf."

I've moved those fallen boughs up the hill nearer the woodpile. I'll cut them down to size when the weather warms up a bit. Yes, I love everything about trees, even raking. The whole family was recently on a road trip and I asked everyone, "What is your favorite living thing on Earth?" Katie chose stones, which prompted a discussion on the nature of rocks. Graham was very specific and chose his dog, Judy, but excluding her he chose sea turtles. And Seamus, having studied abroad for a semester in Thailand, chose the Japanese Maple. I chose trees. When we love something, it isn't about taking the bad with the good, it's all good and there is no burden, which explains why I take up the rake each autumn with pleasure.

With my dearest friends there is no raking at all. It is beyond the reach of my ability to write or speak how fortunate and blessed I am to have a handful of friends that, if they called me right now and asked me to be with them in a time of need, I would close this computer and immediately begin to pack my bag for Big Rapids, Charlotte, Chicago, Milwaukee, Oconomowoc, San Antonio or Des Moines. All ya need is one, and I have seven: Dan, Ken, Chris, Patrick, Mark, Ross, and Tim. And I believe any one of them would be here for me if I asked. It is incredible. If their friendship was currency, I swear I could pay off the national debt and have enough left over to buy a round from Jason at Juniper Moon. Pops Staples, in his song, "Friendship," said it well: "I've been where you are right now, you saw me through it all. I lean on you, now you lean on me and I bet I won't let you fall."

My band of brothers. Some of them don't even know each other, yet every one of them holds a very special key to my heart. And I'm not ashamed to say that it's an exclusive club, not that any of those guys know that. All they need to know is that I love them. I take care of the rest. Those are some of the greatest two words when strung together: take care. When one takes care, nothing is taken for granted, everything is intentional, everything matters.

What gives me a fair amount of longing is the fact that all but one of them live elsewhere. I haven't seen Big Daddy in Charlotte in something like six years. At that rate, I'll see him maybe four more times before I die. And even that is taking an awful lot for granted. And does that mean that I can now count in days the cumulative time I'll spend with my farthest, dearest friends?

All that time whose breath so sweetly lifted the sails of my friendships, from my youth until very recently, now blows one minute a cautionary tale, the next a sigh, as if to say, "Take care!" Well, take care I will, and here resolve to try to see every one of those guys at least once a year, for the rest of my life. Isn't that what we mean when we say, "Be careful out there."?

It's kind of cool that I got to choose my brothers in life. For so long I wished I really had one growing up. To you seven guys and Graz and Jeff, you're the brothers I always dreamed of having and then some.

We learned that our second child was going to be a boy somewhere around Seamus' first birthday. Brothers! I was overjoyed at the thought of experiencing firsthand and getting to be a big part of making beautiful the very thing I so longed for as a boy, brotherhood.

In those days of my son's birth, I was on the fence when it came to Catholicism, and religion in general. Incredulity had my ear, no question, but old ways and patterns of thinking die hard. And so, I was determined to be better than the Father and try my damnedest not to show preferential treatment to one son over another like He did with Cain and Abel. It's a great story, regardless of whether one believes it happened or not. I might be reading it wrong, but I think it's a cautionary tale for fathers.

We must love our children as equally and honestly as we can lest we engender an atmosphere of resentment and insecurity. There were times when I had to take sides, but I always tried to make it a teaching moment, and I don't think my sons ever doubted that I loved them unconditionally no matter what the circumstance. They'll read this someday and hopefully nod their head in agreement and recognition when they do.

For seventeen years the boys lived together under three different roofs. They mostly got along. I think Katie and I did a pretty decent job of letting each boy find himself in their own unique ways. It makes my heart hurt to think how quickly it all came and went.

How can I describe this? How is it so different from how I feel about, say, the days of being a newlywed, which are also long gone? The answer must be in the fact that I can never live again those days with my sons. Katie and I can still make love, dream, go on dates, make plans, travel, make a home, be with our now grown sons, cry, laugh, scratch each other's backs, hear a breath in the middle of the night. But I won't ever dig through several thousand Lego pieces in bins on the basement floor with my boys to make spaceships and fly them around making Star Wars sounds; Graham's took him about 15 minutes to build, Seamus' took an hour or more, but they both flew beautifully in their hands and the crashes were spectacular. Those clamps that I used to secure the blankets of those amazing forts have hardly been touched in years. How many times did a voice shout from the front door to say, "We're going over to Sam's!"? I'd drop everything just to watch them ride their scooters, skateboards, or bikes out the driveway down the street and around the corner until they were out of view. Later it was cars. I was there! I was present 100% in those moments, and I never took them for granted, yet it still hurts to think that those moments are gone forever. No doubt, they are the sweetest of memories and I'm blessed beyond measure to have them. Seventeen years went by quickly.

I have an actor friend named Davida Williams. She has a beautiful way of describing her first born; she refers to her daughter as her first heartbeat. Is there a truer way to describe the connection between a parent and child? Those heartbeats are the essence of the amazing bond I have with my sons today.

And boys, about that neighbor kid that tormented you when you were too young to understand. I'm sorry. I underestimated what evil lived in the heart of a human being. My job was to protect you and I dropped the ball. But here is what I know: none of it was your fault, and the love you own is a million times stronger than that kid. We never talk about it, and we don't have to, but I'm with you to my core and I will listen. I will share. We could probably all use whatever love and healing there is to find there, to pile atop the love we already have.

Parents reading this, be vigilant and trust your instincts beyond what even they suggest.

I have every reason to believe that the next seventeen years will pass at least as quickly as those I shared with the boys at home, presuming I make it to 78. If I'm lucky, my sons and Katie will be with me. With luck and if I live the way I intend, I'll look back and it will hurt, but I'll have no regrets. It will hurt in the way that many beautiful things in life bring me heartache when I look at them; sunsets in the wake of a storm, the way Katie looks with her hair pulled up, green leaves in August, a boy grocery shopping with a mom, an abandoned Little League field, pictures of Katie as a girl with dreams in her heart, an oil can of Foster's Lager, an approaching thunderstorm, the Ogallala exit sign, lilac bushes in June, a theater stage three hours after the final performance.

※

    Sixty-two years ago today, Rita wrote that letter to the priest in Des Moines. It was a little over five months before my birthday. Finding me a home was one thing she did very well in her life. She took tremendous care, and I can say without a doubt that I've known love in my life beyond anything I think she could have imagined for me.

    I've been left to imagine a lot of things about Rita. And unless I come across a diary that I don't know exists, I think I know about all I'm ever going to know about my birth mother.

    My uncle Sean was able to meet his birth mother when he was well into his sixties. Lucky him.

    The Rita of my imagination is, ultimately, a rather sad story. Don't get me wrong, I'm overjoyed to know what I know about her; I will love her and cherish her in my heart until my dying day. But I can't help but feel sorrow for that 26-year-old woman who, in her most vulnerable time, pregnant, with no partner at her side, felt that she couldn't even go to her family for help or comfort; parents, a brother and two sisters, one of whom Rita comforted during her own unplanned pregnancy through to adopting out a couple years before I was born. I can think of a dozen or more reasons why she might feel compelled to hide her pregnancy from her family, aside from Catholic guilt and shame, but at the end of the day it must have been damn lonesome to feel you need to travel over 1,000 miles to have a baby.

Rita's sister has told me that Rita was quick to love, and that she didn't seem to have the best judgment when it came to partners. That would certainly be true of the man who ended Rita's life with two shots to the chest while she read in bed on that summer night in 1987. I'm just glad she kept her name and didn't take his when they married in 1984. She was born Rita Petronella Perquin on June 28, 1934, in Zeist, Netherlands, and that was her name on the day she died.

I've considered going to south Florida to meet Rita's sister and one of my first cousins. We had a Zoom conference call a couple weeks ago and it was delightful to meet them "face to face." We talked a lot about Rita and their memories of her. They scanned some photos I hadn't seen and emailed them to me. It was Rita's sister that mentioned the letters from Rita's friends that she had in her possession, and I sure hope she follows through and mails them to me. Letters or no letters, I'm just starting to feel that maybe I know all that I need to know about my birth mother.

My travels around my hometown take me past the apartment building on Woodland Avenue in the Sherman Hill neighborhood where Rita lived a couple times a month. It's two blocks from Katie's and my favorite cocktail bar, Juniper Moon, and in the neighborhood of two fantastic brew pubs, none of which were around when Rita lived here. About the only thing she'd recognize if she were alive to come visit is the circa

150-year-old cemetery a block away. I like to imagine Rita walking along the narrow lanes and hills therein, pregnant with me, enjoying an early summer evening in the Midwest.

Rita came to town and had her baby. She had her baby, for a little while; me.

She didn't meet the man of her dreams while living here, a man who wouldn't mind that she was having another's child. She also didn't fall in love with her job at Mercy Hospital and decide to stay and make a life here. No, the notes in her file say she was homesick. It's a little strange to feel like I could have been a home for her, a real loving home, that she might be alive today if she had chosen me, that when it was all said and done, I may have been the love of her life. How was she to know? Yeah, it's a strange thought, because at the same time I'm grateful that she moved on. It feels a little selfish to say that. She cut a trail back east the day after I was placed with my mom and dad, which set in motion two separate paths.

One life led to a tragic end at the hands of a man who created dread when he walked in the door: I'm so sorry. To the cowardly son-of-a-bitch who took Rita's life, whose name I know but refuse to mention in these pages, you don't get to end her life at the age of 53. Not in my story. She is alive in me. Right here. Right now.

The other life I've documented in a fair amount of detail in these pages, which led me to this table where I now sit, on a weekday late afternoon as the sun is setting, almost one year after writing the first word, waiting for the love of my life to come home. What a thrill my life is. What a thrill it's been, living where the trees dance.

26
Love

I need to have my eyes checked. I suppose that's better than saying I need to have my head examined, something my mom was fond of telling me in my youth. I need to see…

I was starting to say, "I need to see what's going on with my eyes beyond needing stronger reading glasses." Something stopped me in my tracks.

I need to see?

I'm going to end this memoir by saying I don't need to see. This is as truthful as anything I've written, for the beauty I've seen in Katie, with Katie, is enough to last me the rest of my life. I might miss watching her grow old with me, but I've known her for over 37 years, I can see where this is going and it is adorable. When I look at photos of her as a girl, I feel like I've known her all my life and when I imagine her in thirty more, I fall in love all over again.

I've seen Katie giving birth. Seen her in a wedding gown, in a nightgown, in yoga pants, trying on hats at an art fair with brown hair and gray hair, in hiking boots and leggings, in a sundress backlit by a sunset. Seen her napping on the sofa, planting flowers, singing to her boys, reading in bed, at work, on vacation, at her mom and dad's house where she grew up, with toes in the ocean, gathering pinecones on a mountain trail, collecting stones, riding shotgun in my '63 Ford pickup, dancing, laughing and crying, to name but a few.

I don't want to lose my vision. I'm simply saying that if I did, I wouldn't mourn the loss. At least not in the way I'd miss losing any other sense, by a landslide. Just today, I listened to Yo-Yo Ma play the music of Ennio Morricone on the cello. I would mourn the loss of hearing until the day I died. I'd never get over not being able to hear crickets on a warm summer night or Katie's voice and laughter. But in nearly 62 years, I've seen all that I need to see: Katie. If I'm blessed by grandchildren, well, I've seen my boys. If someone one day says, "That sun setting over the horizon beyond that grove of redwoods is unlike any I've ever seen," I'll beautifully imagine sunsets I've seen from a porch with Katie. I've seen the stars on a moonless night four hundred miles from the nearest lamp. What are they compared to Katie? To me, about a million galaxies too few.

At this point, I must cue up the anthem of this tale. It is the song I danced to a few dozen times with my baby sons in my arms and a few dozen more times with my bride in my arms. It has elevated me to tears more times than I can count. Take me home, Van Morrison, with "Have I Told You Lately."

I'd like to think that what I've written is a love story. It's about how I learned to love myself and be comfortable with myself; only then was I able to love the way I knew I could, the way I always felt was possible. When I was eight or nine years old, I gave a daisy ring to a girl in my class named Damianne, who I remember as kind and beautiful, with long blonde hair. It couldn't have cost me more than fifty cents in 1969. Of course, I didn't know what love meant then, but I felt something that resembled the higher calling I'm certain resided in my being even at the age of nine. From my earliest days I yearned for love.

It's a love story to Rita, and maybe even the birth mothers who read this and simply wonder what ever happened to the boy or girl they let go of. To you I offer this tale of ultimate understanding and gratitude free from judgment. If it's an option, consider reaching out to them. Your story is important, too. You choose the terms.

It's a love story to my mom and dad; the first ones to choose me and from whom I first heard the words, "This is your home, Tommy." What a home. What an amazing garden in which to grow. I spent my entire life as a dad trying to be the best of both in one.

Most of all, it's a love song to sing, to those who want to know me, of how spectacularly beautiful a woman Katie is. My forever bride and mom to our boys, Katie is what the universe gave me when I stood on the coast of Ireland screaming for home and the wind and mist kissed my face and soaked me to the skin. In the springtime of my dreams, she was there whispering to my heart what was possible in life and love.

It sounds magical, but there is no magic in this love. It was fought for in the forsaken solitude of a wanderer; it is the strongest choice, the most noble surrender, the incessant commitment, and when shared, it is a pas de deux that honors the bewondered focus of our first steps and the sublime grace of our last.

For so long I tortured myself with the belief that I had to do something amazing with my life to be worthy of the chance I was given by being born and adopted into such grace and love. In the writing of this memoir, I've realized that I've done it; I've loved and I am loved! I am a good friend and I have men I consider brothers. All the other things I want to do, write the one-man Whitman play, play the guitar better, I'm off to do now.

I love Katie. She is THE true love of my life. My home. And if home is that place one longs for from the very beginning, from the first spark, from birth, in the becoming, then Rita, mom, dad, Seamus, Graham and Katie, I'm there.

CPSIA information can be obtained
at www.ICGtesting.com
Printed in the USA
LVHW051524170723
752374LV00010B/94